Essential SQA Exam Practice

Questions & Papers

National 5 English Practice Questions & Exam Papers

Practise **exam-style questions** for every question type

Complete **2 practice papers** that mirror the real SQA exams

Brian Johnston

Hodder Gibson
AN HACHETTE UK COMPANY

The Publishers would like to thank the following for permission to reproduce copyright material.

Acknowledgements

Pp 1–2 the article 'Why Didn't People Smile in Old Photographs? You Asked Google – and Here's the Answer', by Jonathan Jones in the *Guardian*, August 12, 2015, Copyright © Guardian News & Media Ltd 2019; **p.2** the article 'Stop our oceans choking on a plastic overdose' The FT, April 22, 2018 (Financial Times/FT.com). Used under licence from the Financial Times. All rights reserved; **pp 11, 33–34** and **53–54** extracts from *Sailmaker* by Alan Spence, reproduced by permission of Hodder Education; **pp 13, 37** and **56** extracts from *The Cone-Gatherers*, reprinted with permission of Canongate Books Ltd © Robin Jenkins 2004; **p.15** extract from 'Mrs Midas' copyright © Carol Ann Duffy. Reproduced with permission of the Licensor through PLSClear; **pp 29–30** the article 'Sport will continue to transcend the ages' by Matthew Syed, taken from *The Times* August 12, 2015. Used with permission from The Times/News Licensing; **pp 31–32** and **51–52** extracts from *Bold Girls* by Rona Munro, used with permission from Nick Hern Books Ltd; **pp 35** and **55** extracts from *Tally's Blood* by Ann Marie Di Mambro, reproduced by permission of Ann Marie Di Mambro/Hodder Education (first published by Learning and Teaching Scotland, 2002, then by Education Scotland); **pp 38** and **58** extracts from *The Testament of Gideon Mack* © James Robertson, reproduced by permission of Penguin Books Ltd; **p.39** and **p.59** extracts from *Dr Jekyll and Mr Hyde* by Robert Louis Stevenson. Public domain; **p.40**, extract from 'The Telegram' and **p.60** extract from 'Mother and Son' by Ian Crichton Smith, from *The Red Door: The Complete English Stories 1949–76*, published by Birlinn. Reproduced with permission of the Licensor through PLSClear; **p.41** extract from 'Hieroglyphics' and **pp 61–62** extract from 'Away in a Manger', taken from *Hieroglyphics: and Other Stories* © Anne Donovan 2001. Reprinted with permission of Canongate Books Ltd; **p.42** 'Originally' and **p.63** 'The Way My Mother Speaks' taken from *New Selected Poems 1984–2004* (Picador 2011). Copyright © Carol Ann Duffy. Reproduced by permission of the author c/o Rogers, Coleridge & White Ltd, 20 Powis Mews, London W11 1JN; **p.43** extract from 'In the Snackbar' and **p.65** 'Glasgow 5 March 1971' by Edwin Morgan, taken from *New Selected Poems*, reproduced by permission Carcanet Press Limited; **p.45** 'Assisi' and **p.66** 'Basking Shark' by Norman MacCaig, from *The Poems of Norman MacCaig*, published by Polygon (Birlinn). Reproduced with permission of the Licensor through PLSClear; **p.46** 'Keeping Orchids' and **p.67** 'Lucozade' by Jackie Kay, taken from *Darling: New & Selected Poems* (Bloodaxe Books, 2007) reprinted by permission of Bloodaxe Books on behalf of the author; **pp 49–50**, extract adapted from the article 'The Real Price of Gold' by Brook Larmer in *National Geographic Magazine* (2009), Volume 215, Issue 1. Used by permission National Geographic Society.

Every effort has been made to trace all copyright holders, but if any have been inadvertently overlooked, the Publishers will be pleased to make the necessary arrangements at the first opportunity.

Although every effort has been made to ensure that website addresses are correct at time of going to press, Hodder Gibson cannot be held responsible for the content of any website mentioned in this book. It is sometimes possible to find a relocated web page by typing in the address of the home page for a website in the URL window of your browser.

Hachette UK's policy is to use papers that are natural, renewable and recyclable products and made from wood grown in well-managed forests and other controlled sources. The logging and manufacturing processes are expected to conform to the environmental regulations of the country of origin.

Orders: please contact Bookpoint Ltd, 130 Park Drive, Milton Park, Abingdon, Oxon OX14 4SE. Telephone: (44) 01235 827827. Fax: (44) 01235 400401. Email education@bookpoint.co.uk. Lines are open from 9 a.m. to 5 p.m., Monday to Friday, with a 24-hour message answering service. Visit our website at www.hoddereducation.co.uk. If you have queries or questions that aren't about an order you can contact us at hoddergibson@hodder.co.uk.

© Brian Johnston 2019

First published in 2019 by
Hodder Gibson, an imprint of Hodder Education
An Hachette UK Company
211 St Vincent Street
Glasgow, G2 5QY

Impression number	5	4	3	2	1
Year	2023	2022	2021	2020	2019

Typeset in India by Aptara Inc.

Printed and bound by CPI Group (UK) Ltd, Croydon CR0 4YY

A catalogue record for this title is available from the British Library.

ISBN: 978 1 5104 7186 3

SCOTLAND EXCEL

We are an approved supplier on the Scotland Excel framework.

Schools can find us on their procurement system as:

Hodder & Stoughton Limited t/a Hodder Gibson.

CONTENTS

INTRODUCTION

National 5 English

Welcome to Essential SQA Exam Practice for National 5 English. The aim of this book is to prepare you for the National 5 English exam by progressively building your skills in understanding and answering exam questions. You will find advice on the different question types that you will encounter in the exam papers, as well as model answers, Practice Papers and marking schemes.

To gain the most out of this book, it is recommended that you work your way through all the exercises. However, if you need to focus on certain skills as a matter of priority, you can find these areas in the book and work on those first. It is important to note that this book contains a number of articles and passages from a variety of Scottish texts. It would benefit you greatly to familiarise yourself with these before attempting to answer any questions.

Structure of the book

The materials included in this book are in two sections:

1 Practice Questions
2 Practice Papers

By working through Section 1, you will build up the necessary skills to successfully answer the practice examination questions in Section 2.

Practice Questions

This section outlines the different question types that you will be asked in the Reading for Understanding, Analysis and Evaluation paper, as well as looking at the types of questions you will be asked in the Scottish Set Text Section of the Critical Reading Paper. The questions are arranged by type and will look at the key areas and skills that will be assessed. This section can be picked up at any time, and you can focus on any areas you may be finding difficult. You will be given handy hints and tips to hone your skills throughout this section.

How to answer

Each set of questions in this section starts with a short commentary, which describes the question type and gives some support in answering it. The commentary built into the answers for the Practice Papers will help too.

Practice Papers

This section contains two full practice exam papers worth a total of 70 marks each. These will give you experience in answering the types of questions that will appear in the final exam. These papers have been designed to be very similar to a typical National 5 question paper. In each Practice Paper, you will find a Reading for Understanding, Analysis and Evaluation paper worth 30 marks and a Critical Reading paper that is worth 40 marks. When you have completed them, you can look at the accompanying marking instructions, which will give you further guidance on how to improve your exam skills.

The course

The National 5 English course is designed to afford you opportunities to develop and apply key language skills in reading, writing, listening and talking. The National 5 course aims to enable you to develop the ability to:

▶ listen, talk, read and write as appropriate to purpose, audience and context

▶ understand, analyse and evaluate texts, including Scottish texts, as appropriate to purpose and audience in the contexts of literature, language and media

▶ create and produce texts, as appropriate to purpose and audience and context

▶ apply knowledge and understanding of language.

By engaging with a range of texts across a variety of genres, you will improve your skills in communication, develop your ability to think critically and learn skills that will enhance your creativity and imagination. The acquisition of these skills will allow you not only to be successful in the examination but, because of the integral nature of them, they will be useful throughout your life.

How the award is graded

This course is assessed through coursework and exams. The exam consists of two papers: Reading for Understanding, Analysis and Evaluation, and Critical Reading. You will also produce a portfolio of writing. Although this is marked externally by SQA, you will work on your portfolio throughout the year with guidance from your teacher. You will need to produce two pieces of writing: one broadly creative in nature and the other broadly discursive. Combined, they are worth 30% of your final grade.

Finally, there is there is a mandatory performance-spoken language assessment. This will be internally assessed by your teacher. This does not count towards your final grade, but you must achieve the requirements before you can receive a final overall grade.

The table below outlines the timings and weightings for each element of assessment.

Component	Time	Percentage
Reading for Understanding, Analysis and Evaluation	1 hour	30%
Critical Reading	1 hour and 30 minutes	40%
Portfolio of writing	Developed throughout the course and final submission to SQA prior to the final exam	30%
Spoken language assessment	Developed throughout the course and internally assessed	Achieved/not achieved

The exams

Reading for Understanding, Analysis and Evaluation

▶ Exam time: 1 hour

▶ Total marks: 30

▶ Weighting in final grade: 30%

▶ What you have to do: read an article and answer questions about it.

This part of the exam involves reading an unseen non-fiction text. The questions are designed to test your ability on how well you can **understand**, **analyse** and **evaluate** the text. You will see these question types are indicated in the student margin of example questions.

Many of the passages used in the exam come from pieces of quality journalism, so it is a good idea that you become familiar with this type of writing before the exam. You can do this by regularly reading newspapers such as *The Guardian*, the *Herald* or *The Times*. If you do this habitually then you will improve your knowledge and understanding of language, which will also benefit your writing and overall word power.

Critical Reading

▶ Exam time: 1 hour and 30 minutes

▶ Total marks: 40

▶ Weighting in final grade: 40%

▶ What you have to do: Section 1: read an extract from one of the Scottish Set Texts which are set for National 5 and answer questions; Section 2: write an essay about a work of literature you have studied during your course.

Section 1

To gain the full 12 marks in the first few questions, you will need to use some of the same skills you use in the RUAE part of the exam, such as analysis of word choice, imagery and sentence structure. To gain the full 8 marks in the second question of Section 1, you will need to make connections between the extract and the rest of the text (drama and novels) or between the extract and another text by the same writer (short stories and poems). The examiner will be looking for three things:

▶ Identification of 'commonality' as specified in the question (for 2 marks)

▶ At least one relevant reference to and comment on the extract (for 2 marks)

▶ At least two relevant references to and comments on the rest of the text (or other poems or short stories) (for 4 marks).

Your answer to this question can be written in bullet points or using a number of linked statements. Good marks can be obtained using either approach. You should decide which method you are most comfortable with and use it confidently.

Section 2

The Critical Essay section is worth 20 marks and you have the choice of answering on the following genres: Drama, Prose, Poetry, Film and Television Drama, or Language. You will have studied at least one of these genres and have practised essay writing in class. You should only attempt one question, and you must choose a question on a different genre from that chosen in Section 1. The Critical Essay is marked holistically and assessed on how well you make a genuine attempt to respond to literature you have studied. There are a range of marks available, but in order to do well your essay should be detailed and relevant.

To prepare for this part of the exam, you should revise the themes and central concerns of the text(s) you have studied, and the techniques used by the writer(s). You must use appropriate quotations to support your answer and you need to recall them from memory in the exam. Writing flashcards, creating a recording or mind-maps can help you learn your quotations. Find a method that works for you and stick with it. It's important to have lots of ideas about at least one of the texts you have studied and use these to tackle the question you choose from the exam paper. You mustn't use the exam question as an excuse to use an answer you've prepared in advance. Just remember to:

▶ **structure** your essay carefully

▶ stay **relevant** to the question

▶ show your **understanding** of **the central ideas** and **themes**

▶ show your **understanding** of **techniques used by the writer**

▶ show your **knowledge** of the text by using appropriate **quotations** or **short explanations of key points in the text**.

The supplementary marking grid below shows you how Critical Essays are graded. You can refer back to this grid during your revision and after you have attempted the practice Critical Essay sections in this book. You can download a Revision Calendar to use as part of your studies from our website at www.hoddergibson.co.uk/ESEP-extras

Good study habits are essential to success. By working through the two sections in this book, you will equip yourself with the necessary skills to pass the National 5 English exam. If you feel prepared, you will be able to enter the exam hall feeling positive. Even if you find yourself unsure of how to answer a question, trust your instincts and try your best. Good luck!

Supplementary marking grid

	Marks 20–18	Marks 17–14	Marks 13–10	Marks 9–5	Marks 4–0
The critical essay demonstrates	▲ a high degree of familiarity with the text as a whole ▲ very good understanding of the central concerns of the text ▲ a line of thought that is consistently relevant to the task	▲ familiarity with the text as a whole ▲ good understanding of the central concerns of the text ▲ a line of thought that is relevant to the task	▲ some familiarity with the text as a whole ▲ some understanding of the central concerns of the text ▲ a line of thought that is mostly relevant to the task	▲ familiarity with some aspects of the text ▲ an attempt at a line of thought but this may lack relevance to the task	Although such essays should be rare, in this category, the critical essay will demonstrate one or more of the following: ▲ it contains numerous errors in spelling/grammar/punctuation/sentence construction/paragraphing ▲ knowledge and understanding of the text(s) are not used to answer the question ▲ any analysis and evaluation attempted are unconvincing ▲ the answer is simply too thin
Analysis of the text demonstrates	▲ thorough awareness of the writer's techniques, through analysis, making confident use of critical terminology ▲ very detailed/thoughtful explanation of stylistic devices supported by a range of well-chosen references and/or quotations	▲ sound awareness of the writer's techniques through analysis, making good use of critical terminology ▲ detailed explanation of stylistic devices supported by appropriate references and/or quotations	▲ an awareness of the writer's techniques through analysis, making some use of critical terminology ▲ explanation of stylistic devices supported by some appropriate references and/or quotations	▲ some awareness of the more obvious techniques used by the writer ▲ description of some stylistic devices followed by some reference and/or quotation	
Evaluation of the text is shown through	▲ a well-developed commentary of what has been enjoyed/gained from the text(s), supported by a range of well-chosen references to its relevant features	▲ a reasonably developed commentary of what has been enjoyed/gained from the text(s), supported by appropriate references to its relevant features	▲ some commentary of what has been enjoyed/gained from the text(s), supported by some appropriate references to its relevant features	▲ brief commentary of what has been enjoyed/gained from the text(s), followed by brief reference to its features	
The critical essay	▲ uses language to communicate a line of thought very clearly ▲ uses spelling, grammar, sentence construction and punctuation which are consistently accurate ▲ structures the essay effectively to enhance meaning/purpose ▲ uses paragraphing which is accurate and effective	▲ uses language to communicate a line of thought clearly ▲ uses spelling, grammar, sentence construction and punctuation which are mainly accurate ▲ structures the essay very well ▲ uses paragraphing which is accurate	▲ uses language to communicate a line of thought at first reading ▲ uses spelling, grammar, sentence construction and punctuation which are sufficiently accurate ▲ attempts to structure the essay in an appropriate way ▲ uses paragraphing which is sufficiently accurate	▲ uses language to communicate a line of thought which may be disorganised and/or difficult to follow ▲ makes some errors in spelling/grammar/sentence construction/punctuation ▲ has not structured the essay well ▲ has made some errors in paragraphing	
In summary, the critical essay is	thorough and precise	very detailed and shows some insight	fairly detailed and accurate	lacking in detail and relevance	superficial and/or technically weak

KEY AREA INDEX GRIDS

Reading for Understanding, Analysis and Evaluation

Question type	Command word(s)	Approach	Practice questions in this book	
			Paper 1	Paper 2
Understanding: This type of question is designed to check you understand the ideas, meaning and language of the passage.				
Explain	Explain how	Locate ideas/words/ phrases and paraphrase	1, 2, 5, 6, 8, 9	1, 4, 6
Identify	Identify	Locate ideas/words/ phrases and paraphrase		
Summarise	Summarise	Locate ideas/words/ phrases and paraphrase. Bullet points may help organise your answer		5
Analysis: This type of question is designed to check you can identify specific techniques writers use and comment on how they add to the reader's appreciation of the passage.				
Examples of language	Examples of language, word choice, sentence structure, tone, contrast, imagery	Identify techniques (these may be explicitly asked for or not) by quoting and then comment on how they answer the question.	7	3, 7
Word choice	Word choice, example of language	Quote an example and comment on how the words answer the question. Make reference to connotations.	3, 4	2
Sentence structure	Sentence structure, example of language	Find the techniques of sentence structure that answer the question and explain why they are effective.		
Imagery	Imagery, example of language	Look for metaphors, similes or personification and explain what these mean literally and in the context of the passage/ question.		
Tone	Tone, example of language	Find the words that indicate the tone and explain how they do so.		
Contrast	Contrast, example of language	Identify both sides of the contrast and explain why they contrast, in relation to the question.		
Evaluation: This type of question asks you to consider how well a feature or idea contributes to the overall purpose or argument.				
Usefulness	Effectiveness	In relation to the question, pick examples of content, ideas or language and explain how these work.		9

Critical Reading – Scottish Set Text

Question type	Command word(s)	Approach	Practice questions in this book	
			Paper 1	Paper 2
Own words	Explain, using your own words	Locate ideas/words/phrases and paraphrase.	1a, 5, 14, 21, 22, 23, 26, 27a, 34, 38	3, 6, 7, 11a, 14, 15, 22, 27, 40, 47, 48
Language	Explain how, Referring to example of language	Find the information in the text that answers the question. Quote and then explain in your own words why you have picked it.	1b, 2, 3, 6, 7, 9, 10, 11, 13, 15, 17, 18, 19, 24, 27b, 28, 30, 31, 32, 35, 36, 39, 40, 41, 43, 44, 45, 47b, 48	1, 2, 4, 8, 10, 11b, 13, 16, 18, 19 20, 23, 24, 25, 28, 29, 31, 32a, 32b, 33, 35, 36, 37, 38, 41, 42, 43, 45, 46, 49, 51, 52, 53
8 marker	Referring to this … show how …	Include: 2 marks worth for commonality. From the extract: 2 marks for extract (i.e. 1 × relevant reference to technique or feature or idea (1) 1 × appropriate comment (1)). NB: maximum of 2 marks only for discussion of extract. Elsewhere or other texts: reference to technique or feature or idea (1) 1 × appropriate comment (1) × 2	4, 8, 12, 16, 20, 25, 29, 33, 37, 42, 46, 49	4, 9, 12, 17, 21, 26, 30, 34, 39, 44, 50, 54

Reading for Understanding, Analysis and Evaluation

This section looks at the different question types you can expect to see on the exam paper and will help you to build your reading skills. Below you will see two articles: *Why didn't people smile in old photos?* and *Stop our oceans choking on a plastic overdose*. Read the articles carefully, then move on to read the information about the different question types. Then you can practise exam questions for each question type.

Becoming familiar with the different question types and practising answering them will develop your confidence. The practice questions in this section are organised by question type – **understanding** questions, **analysis** questions and **evaluation** questions. These practice questions will also help you to build your reading skills, which is a vital component of the National 5 course.

Example passage 1

Why didn't people smile in old photos?

From the time that photography was invented in 1839, portraiture (the likeness of a person, especially the face) was at the heart of its appeal. A noticeable feature of these early photographic portraits is that smiles are grimly absent from them. If you look, for example, at a famous old photograph of a young girl taken in 1852, you see her posed for the camera, her head slightly turned, giving the lens a steady, confident, unsmiling look. She is
5   preserved forever as a very serious girl indeed.

That severity is everywhere in Victorian photographs. Charles Darwin, by all accounts a warm character and a loving, playful parent, looks frozen in glumness in photographs. In Julia Margaret Cameron's great 1867 portrait of the astronomer John Frederick William Herschel, his deep melancholy introspection and wild hair kissed by the light give him the air of a Shakespearean tragic hero.

10 Why did our ancestors, from unknown sitters for family portraits to the great and famous, become so mirthless in front of the lens? The apparently obvious answer is that they are freezing their faces in order to keep still for the long exposure times, but you don't have to look very long at these unsmiling old photos to see how incomplete that answer is. In Julia Margaret Cameron's portrait of the poet Tennyson, he broods and dreams, his face a shadowed mask of genius. This is not simply a technical quirk. It's an aesthetic and emotional choice.

15 People in the past were not necessarily more gloomy than we are. They did not go around in a perpetual state of sorrow – though they might be forgiven for doing so, in a world with much higher mortality rates than in the west today, and medicine that was puny indeed by our standards. In fact, the Victorians had a sense of humour even about the darkest aspects of their society. Jerome K Jerome's book *Three Men in a Boat* is a fascinating insight into the Victorian sense of humour – it's rollicking and irreverent. When the narrator drinks some water
20 from the river Thames, his friends chaff him that he will probably catch cholera. It's a startling joke to make in 1889 just a few decades after cholera had ravaged London. Chaucer wrote *The Canterbury Tales*, which can still raise laughs today, in the fourteenth century, the century of the Black Death and the Hundred Years War. Jane Austen found plenty to giggle about in the era of the Napoleonic wars.

Laughter and jollity were not just common in the past but institutionalised far more than they are today, from
25 medieval carnivals in which entire communities indulged in riotous comic antics to Georgian printshops where people gathered to look at the latest funnies. Far from suppressing festivals and fun, the Victorians, who invented photography, also created Christmas as the secular feast it is today.

So the severity of people in 19th-century photographs cannot be evidence of generalised gloom and depression. This was not a society in permanent despair. Instead, the true answer has to do with attitudes to
30 portraiture itself.

People who posed for early photographs, from earnest middle-class families recording their status to celebrities captured by the lens, understood it as a significant moment. Photography was still rare. Having your picture taken was not something that happened every day. For many people it might be a once-in-a-lifetime experience.

Posing for the camera, in other words, did not seem that different from having your portrait painted. It was
35 cheaper, quicker (even with those slow exposure times) and meant that people who never had a chance to be painted could now be portrayed; but people seem to have taken it seriously in the same way they would a painted portrait. This was not a 'snap'. Like a portrait painting, it was intended as a timeless record of a person.

Oil portraits of long ago are not that packed with smiles, either. Rembrandt's portraits would look very different if everyone was smiling in them. In fact, they are full of the consciousness of mortality and the mystery of
40 existence – nothing to smile about there. Look at the intimately serious portraits painted by Velazquez or Titian or indeed most of the painted portraits in any museum and there aren't many smiley faces.

For the most part, melancholy and introspection haunt the oil portrait and this sense of the seriousness of life passes on from painting into early photography, which, I think, makes the old photographs so much more moving than modern ones. For what still survives in Victorian photography is the grandeur and gravitas of
45 traditional portraiture.

Today, we take so many smiling snaps that the idea of anyone finding true depth and poetry in most of them is absurd. Photos are about being social. We want to communicate ourselves as happy social people. So we smile, laugh and cavort in endless and endlessly shared selfies. A grinning selfie is the opposite of a serious portrait. It's just a momentary performance of happiness. It has zero profundity and therefore zero artistic value. As a
50 human document it is disturbingly throwaway. (In fact, not even solid enough to throw away – just press delete).

How beautiful and haunting old photographs are in comparison with our silly selfies. Those unsmiling people probably had as much fun as we do, if not more. But they felt no hysterical need to prove it with pictures. Instead, when they posed for a photograph, they thought about time, death and memory. The presence of those grave realities in old photographs makes them worth far more than our inanely happy Instagram snaps.

Example passage 2

Stop our oceans choking on a plastic overdose

Rarely has a global environmental issue aroused public and political concern more rapidly than plastic pollution of the oceans. Images of litter-coated beaches on once idyllic islands — and sea creatures entangled in lethal debris or poisoned by plastic pieces mistaken for morsels of food — are forcing governments and companies into overdue action to reduce the estimated 8m tonnes of waste plastic that find their way into the oceans every
5 year. So too is alarm about the almost invisible threat of tiny microplastic particles and fibres, resulting mainly from the disintegration of larger items, which may pose a toxic time bomb for marine life and eventually humans too.

Policymakers should therefore focus their efforts on rapidly reducing the flow of fresh material into the ocean, by increasing recycling and restricting non-essential uses of plastics. This will require a huge change in behaviour by the world's consumers, pushed by government regulations such as mandatory deposits
10 on plastic bottles, charges for plastic bags and coffee cups, and bans on certain products, such as the one proposed last week by Theresa May, UK prime minister, on plastic straws and cotton buds. At the same time the manufacturing and retail sectors must go further and faster than most have announced so far to phase out unnecessary plastic packaging.

Even so, millions of tonnes of plastic will still need recycling every year for the time being. Product designers
15 have an important role to play in the creation of a "circular economy", making it simpler to separate different components at the end of their life and identify different plastic ingredients.

A priority for research is to improve recycling technology. A hint of what might be possible came last week when an international team announced the discovery of an enzyme that can break down PET, the polymer used to make bottles; it was extracted from bacteria evolving to eat waste plastic in Japan. The next big EU research
20 programme could lead the way by adopting plastic-free oceans as a "grand challenge".

All these actions must take place on a global scale, since most plastic reaches the sea from the developing world and particularly from the larger Asian economies. That may mean transferring money and even technology to help poorer countries handle the huge recycling job that they face.

Fortunately plastic pollution, unlike climate change, is an environmental cause without a vociferous band of
25 sceptics denying the scientific consensus that action is needed urgently. In that respect it is more like the 1980s crisis over the destruction of the protective ozone layer in the upper atmosphere. Then international agreement quickly banned the non-essential use of ozone-destroying CFC chemicals in aerosols, fridges and elsewhere. The battle against unnecessary plastics will not be so straightforward but we can draw some encouragement from successful phase-out of CFCs 30 years ago.

Now let's look at the different question types and how we can answer them.

Question type: Understanding

≫ HOW TO ANSWER

The most common question you will be asked in the exam is to explain a point the writer makes **using your own words**. This demonstrates your understanding of an extract. At least half of the 30 marks available will be made up of this type of question. Many students often find this type of question challenging because of a limited vocabulary, but this should not be the case if you build up your reading and practise regularly. If you do build your vocabulary in this way, you will find these questions straightforward as they are essentially testing your knowledge of what the writer is saying and what the passage is about. If the writer does not explicitly state their ideas, you will need to use your inference skills.

Understanding questions often use key phrases such as:

► Explain in your own words …
► Identify, in your own words as far as possible …
► Summarise, in your own words as far as possible …

Another important type of understanding question is the **summarising** question. Not only is this an important exam skill but one that will stand you in good stead in the future. In this kind of question, you are expected to look at a specific part of the passage and summarise the main points the writer is making. You will need to select key information and succinctly put it into your own words.

Top Tip!

Remember, these types of questions require you to rephrase key ideas and/or phrases and expressions using your own words. You should not quote from the passage or try to discuss any of the language features used. You are being asked to show your **understanding** by writing the ideas of the passage in a different way.

Top Tip!

It is useful in this kind of question to bullet point your answer.

Now try writing your own responses to these practice questions. You will need to refer *to Why didn't people smile in old photos?*

1 Look at lines 1–11. Explain **in your own words** two key points the writer is making about early photographic portraits.

MARKS	STUDENT MARGIN
2	Understanding

Hint!

Focus on what the question asks you to do. Here, it guides you to the relevant lines then asks you to explain two points the writer is making. Look at these lines and try to put them **into your own words**. You can see the question is worth two marks, so you must write down two separate points. You may find it useful to bullet point your answers for each point you make.

Take a common-sense approach when changing words. For example, adjectives, verbs and adverbs are usually easy to change. You can replace them with synonyms – words that mean the same, or very *nearly* the same, thing. There are some words you won't be able to change, such as proper nouns.

A possible answer may look like this:

→ People did not smile in old photographs.
→ People also look very stern and sombre.

	MARKS	STUDENT MARGIN

2 Look at lines 19–34. Summarise, **in your own words** as far as possible, the evidence the writer gives that 'People in the past were not necessarily more gloomy than we are'.

You should make **five** key points in your answer.

5   Understanding

> ## Hint!
> You have been directed to the relevant section and asked to make **five** points. Each point will need to be concisely paraphrased **into your own words**. Bullet points should ensure that you have written enough detail for the available marks.

Now try writing your own responses to these practice questions. You will need to refer to *Stop our oceans choking on a plastic overdose*.

1 Look at lines 1–8. Explain **in your own words** why plastic pollution has become a global concern.

You should make **three** key points in your answer.

3   Understanding

2 Look at lines 18–24. Summarise, **in your own words** as far as possible, the action that we need to take to reduce plastic use.

You should make **five** key points in your answer.

5   Understanding

You should now feel more confident in dealing with understanding questions. Remember, the best way of dealing with own word questions is to have an extended and varied vocabulary, and the best way of gaining this is by reading.

Question type: Analysis

≫ HOW TO ANSWER

Analysis questions assess your ability to analyse how writers use style and language to create particular effects. You should **quote** from the text to support your explanation of the effects created by the language. 'Language' is a general term used by the SQA to refer to all aspects of style, including word choice, imagery, structure and tone. At National 5 level you are awarded a mark for a correct selection of a writer's technique. You can download a helpful glossary of common techniques used by writers that will help you in your revision.

Analysis questions use key phrases such as:

▶ Explain how one example of the writer's use of language …
▶ Explain how one example of the writer's use of sentence structure …
▶ Explain how two examples of the writer's word choice …
▶ Explain how the writer's use of language …
▶ Explain fully why the simile … is effective …
▶ By referring to two language features, explain how the writer makes clear …

The number of marks will guide how much you will need to write. For example, a four-mark question will need two examples with analytical comments for each.

▶ **Word choice** – only pick out single words or short expressions to analyse. You need to be specific so do not select whole sentences to comment on. Analytical comments about the connotations or associations will help.
▶ **Imagery** – look out for examples of simile, metaphors or personification. You need to explain what two things are being compared and why this is effective in the context of the passage.
▶ **Sentence structure** – look out for common features such as lists, repetition, use of short sentences and use of questions. You will need to quote the part that you are referring to and explain the effect it has on the reader.
▶ **Use of contrast** – look for two very different things or ideas being put together. You will look at both sides of the contrast and explain the effect.
▶ **Tone** – look out for the writer's attitude being expressed. The tone is created through the language that the writer uses. Imagining the passage being read aloud often helps to pick up the writer's attitude about the subject.

The key command words in analysis questions are **how** or **why**. Sometimes, language questions will ask you to look at two different language techniques. They may have the following phrase after the question: *You should refer to two different features such as word choice, imagery or sentence structure.*

Firstly, look at the lines specified in the question and identify the techniques used by the writer.

Secondly, identify the technique that you will use as an example and quote it in your answer. Thirdly, explain how the example that you have chosen creates an effect on the reader.

Top Tip!
Underlining or highlighting the lines can help.

Now try writing your own responses to these practice questions. You will need to refer to *Why didn't people smile in old photos?*

	MARKS	STUDENT MARGIN

3 Look at lines 1–4. Explain how **two** examples of the writer's word choice make clear his liking for old photographs.

MARKS: **4** — Analysis

> ## Hint!
> Remember to pay attention to what the question is asking you to do, and how many marks are available. At National 5 level you will achieve a mark for each appropriate selection, and a mark for an appropriate analytical comment. This is a four-mark question, so you must do this twice.
>
> Note that the question asks about the writer's 'liking for old photographs'. This tells you that the words you choose should have positive associations.

4 Look at lines 5–11. Explain how **two** examples of language make clear the writer's dislike of modern photographs.

MARKS: **4** — Analysis

> ## Hint!
> Notice how this question is asking about language. 'Language' is a broad term used by SQA to mean all aspects of writing such as word choice, imagery, sentence structure and tone. This means you need to decide what features to focus on in your answer.
>
> You will achieve one mark for an appropriate reference and one mark for an analytical comment on the reference. This is a four-mark question, so you must do this twice.

Now try two more examples. You will need to refer to *Stop plastic pollution in our oceans*.

3 Look at lines 1–8. Explain how **two** examples of language make it clear that action against plastic pollution is needed.

MARKS: **4** — Analysis

> ## Hint!
> This question is asking for **two** examples of language used to make it clear that action against plastic pollution is needed. You will need to give your example then write an analytical comment. As this question is worth 4 marks, you need to do this twice.

4 Look at lines 12–25. By referring to **two** language features, explain how the writer makes clear the extent of plastic pollution.
You should refer to two different features such as word choice, imagery or sentence structure.

MARKS: **4** — Analysis

> ## Hint!
> This is an interesting question because you need to refer to two **different** features and comment on them in order to achieve full marks. This means that you could not comment on, for example, two examples of imagery and gain full marks. Again, this highlights how important it is to read the question very closely and be sure you know what is being asked of you before you put pen to paper.
>
> You approach this type of question in exactly the same way as the previous analysis questions by making a selection and making an analytical comment. This question is for four marks so you need to do this twice.

Question type: Evaluation

>> HOW TO ANSWER

Evaluation questions require you to use both your understanding and analysis skills to evaluate how well or how effectively you think the writer has used different language features to achieve the purpose of the passage. The SQA have selected the passages because of their effectiveness so your opinion and comment should reflect this.

The two main types of evaluation questions are:

▶ evaluating the effectiveness of introductions
▶ evaluating the effectiveness of conclusions.

Similarly, in evaluating the effectiveness of a conclusion, you should consider the following points:

1   Does it sum up the main points?
2   Does it restate the writer's point of view?
3   Does it link back to the introduction?
4   Does it use word choice/imagery from the introduction or throughout the passage?
5   Does it conclude in some other memorable way? For example, using a rhetorical question or powerful image.

For both effective introduction and conclusion questions, you need to have a clear idea of what the writer has tried to achieve and how the techniques used have helped them achieve their purpose. Therefore, when you answer evaluation questions you are expected to make a judgement about how successful the writer has been.

Top Tip!

When you are dealing with evaluation questions, it is essential that you select an example and then show how it connects with a point or technique used earlier in the passage. It is important that your comment connects to the passage as a whole.

	MARKS	STUDENT MARGIN

Now try writing your own responses to these practice questions. You will need to refer to *Why didn't people smile in old photos?*

5   Look at lines 1–5. Explain fully how the opening paragraph is an effective introduction.

| | 2 | Evaluation |

Hint!

This question asks you to explain how a feature, idea or technique adds to the effectiveness of the introduction. You need to quote an example from the introduction and then explain how it generates interest in the reader.

6   Look at lines 51–54. Select any expression from these lines and explain how it contributes to the passage's effective conclusion.

| | 2 | Evaluation |

Hint!

This question asks you to choose an expression from the last paragraph and show how this relates back to a previous feature, idea or technique. You need to quote an example and explain how it adds to the effective conclusion.

MARKS | STUDENT MARGIN

Now let's try another two examples. You will need to refer to *Stop our oceans choking on a plastic overdose.*

5 Look at lines 1–6. Explain fully how the opening paragraph is an effective introduction.

2 — Evaluation

> ### Hint!
> Look out for features of language that grab the reader's attention in an introduction. Consider:
> → Does it introduce the main points?
> → Does it make clear the writer's point of view?
> → Does it hook the reader with a clever technique?
>
> You need to **quote** and **explain** how effective you think the writer has been at whatever point you make.

6 Look at lines 24–29. Select any expression from these lines and explain how it contributes to the passage's effective conclusion.

2 — Evaluation

> ### Hint!
> In evaluating the effectiveness of a conclusion, you should consider the following points:
> → Does it sum up the main points?
> → Does it restate the writer's point of view?
> → Does it link back to the introduction?
> → Does it use word choice/imagery from the introduction or throughout the passage?
> → Does it conclude in some other memorable way? For example, using a rhetorical question or powerful image.
>
> When you are dealing with this type of question, it is essential that you select an example and then show how it connects with a point or technique used earlier in the passage. It is important that your comment connects to the passage as a whole.
>
> You should hopefully be feeling confident in your reading for Understanding, Analysis and Evaluation skills. The next section will deal with Critical Reading, and the good news is that the skills that you have worked on in this section will come in handy in this paper, too!

2028

Critical Reading

The Critical Reading paper of the National 5 exam is in two parts and lasts for 1 hour and 30 minutes. The Scottish Set Text section requires you to answer questions on a Scottish author that you will have studied in class in detail with your teacher. This is worth 20 marks. The Critical Essay section is worth a further 20 marks and you have the choice of answering on the following genres: Drama, Prose, Poetry, Film and Television Drama, or Language. You will have studied at least one of these genres in class and have practised essay writing, with your teacher giving you feedback. You should only attempt one Critical Essay.

It is important to point out that your answer in the Critical Essay section **must** be from a different **genre** to your Scottish Set Text answers. You cannot use the same genre for both Section 1 and Section 2. In other words, if you have studied the play *Sailmaker*, you could not go on and write an essay on the plays *Bold Girls* or *Tally's Blood*. You should spend approximately 45 minutes on each section of the Critical Reading paper.

Many of the skills you need to be successful in the Critical Reading paper draw heavily on the understanding, analysis and evaluation skills you developed in Section 1 of this book and the RUAE papers that you will have practised.

The Scottish Set Text

The Scottish Set Text involves you studying literature (drama, prose or poetry) by a Scottish author from a list prescribed by the SQA. This list is refreshed every few years but the current texts you can study at National 5 level are as follows:

Drama

▶ *Bold Girls* by Rona Munro

▶ *Sailmaker* by Alan Spence

▶ *Tally's Blood* by Ann Marie di Mambro

Prose

▶ Short stories by Iain Crichton Smith: *The Red Door, The Telegram, Mother and Son, Home*

▶ *The Cone-Gatherers* by Robin Jenkins

▶ *Dr Jekyll and Mr Hyde* by Robert Louis Stevenson

▶ Short stories by Anne Donovan: *All that Glisters, Away in a Manger, Dear Santa, Hieroglyphics*

▶ *The Testament of Gideon Mack* by James Robertson

> **Hint!**
>
> Before you begin answering the questions it is important to:
>
> → Read the poem/excerpt through before you start, even if you know it well
>
> → Read the questions **carefully**. This will ensure you know exactly what is being asked
>
> → Check how many marks each question is worth and think about how these marks will be allocated.

Poetry

▶ Carol Ann Duffy: *War Photographer, Valentine, Originally, Mrs Midas, In Mrs Tilscher's Class, The Way My Mother Speaks*

▶ Norman MacCaig: *Assisi, Visiting Hour, Aunt Julia, Basking Shark, Hotel Room, 12th Floor, Brooklyn Cop*

▶ Edwin Morgan: *In the Snack-bar, Trio, Good Friday, Winter, Glasgow 5 March 1971, Glasgow Sonnet i*

▶ Jackie Kay: *My Grandmother's Houses, Lucozade, Gap Year, Keeping Orchids, Old Tongue, Whilst Leila Sleeps*

You will study at least one of the authors on the list in detail with your English teacher, who will prepare you for this section of the Critical Reading paper. In the Scottish Set Text section of the exam, you will be asked to read an extract from a text you have studied in class and then answer questions on it. This part of the exam is worth 20 marks. The first 12 marks are about the extract that is published in the exam paper, while the final 8-mark question relates to either other poems or short stories, or the text as a whole if you have studied drama or a novel.

The skills you require to be successful here are very similar to the understanding, analysis and evaluation skills you will develop when practising RUAE. The main difference is that these questions are about literature rather than non-fiction. However, the strategies that you adopt to answer the questions will be the same.

Common command words and phrases

As in RUAE, there are certain command words and phrases that will tell you exactly what the examiner is looking for. Look out for common phrases used in exam papers and prepare for how to answer them. The question types below will give you advice on how to answer Scottish Set Text questions.

>> HOW TO ANSWER

Identify two of the main concerns in the text …

Identify is a command word that means find an idea and put it into your own words – unless it asks you to identify a quote or technique. When asked about the main ideas or concerns of the text, show your understanding of the poem or text's story and the main messages and themes it is conveying. You should use your own words as far as possible.

Show how one example of the language helps to clarify or illustrate meaning …

This is an **analysis** question, asking you to focus on the **language**. Like language questions in RUAE, you need to quote from the text to support your answer. You will need to include a relevant quote to gain one mark, and comment on its effect in relation to the question to gain a further mark. The number of marks available will guide your response.

How effective do you find …

This is an **evaluation** question. These questions are asking how well you think the writer has done something. In the same way as RUAE, it is easier to argue that the writer has used language effectively and then show how by quoting a word or technique and commenting on it.

How effective do you find any two aspects of the final stanza as a conclusion to the poem?

This is another **evaluation** question, typically used in reference to poetry. When answering a question that asks you about the conclusion of a poem, you will need to show an understanding of the term 'conclusion' and show how the last lines continue the ideas or language or imagery from the rest of the poem. Generally, conclusions sum up the key ideas of a text and leave us with something to think about.

> ### Top Tip!
>
> Some possible features or ideas that you could comment on include:
> - a continuation of the ideas
> - a continuation of language
> - a continuation of imagery
> - a link or echo of the opening lines
> - a striking or dramatic final line which highlights one of the poem's key ideas
> - the use of rhetorical questions.

The final question

The final question is worth 8 marks. You may choose to answer in bullet points in this final question, or write a number of linked statements. There is no requirement to write a 'mini essay'. It will ask you to compare or contrast the excerpt you have in front of you with at least one other text you have studied by the same writer, or the rest of the play or novel if you have studied drama or a novel.

Marks are allocated according to your ability to identify aspects of commonality. This means you need to analyse the extract and show how it relates to ideas and language features found elsewhere in your chosen text or texts. The marks are allocated as follows:

▶ Up to 2 marks can be achieved for identifying elements of commonality as identified in the question.

▶ A further 2 marks can be achieved for reference to the extract given. You should refer to the extract you have been given in relation to the question.

▶ 4 additional marks can be awarded for similar references to at least one other text/part of the text by the writer in relation to the question. This means that you will make a relevant reference to technique, idea or feature and make an appropriate comment.

We will now look at some examples of Scottish Set Text questions. The texts we will look at are *Sailmaker* by Alan Spence; *The Cone-Gatherers* by Robin Jenkins and an extract from *Mrs Midas* by Carol Ann Duffy.

Drama

Sailmaker by Alan Spence

The extract is from the closing moments of Act One.

(DAVIE *and* BILLY *enter, opposite sides of stage*)

	BILLY:	What's up wi your face?

(DAVIE *shakes head*)

		What's the matter?
5	DAVIE:	Ah just got ma jotters. Week's notice.
	BILLY:	Jesus Christ! What for?
	DAVIE:	Ach! They're saying the book's a dead loss. They're gonnae shut it awthegether. Put the sheriff's officers on tae the folk that still owe money.
	BILLY:	Bastards.
10	DAVIE:	Getting that doin just finished it. Losin the money an the ledgers an everythin.
	BILLY:	But that wasnae your fault!
	DAVIE:	Try tellin *them* that! So that's me. Scrubbed. Again. Laid off. Redundant. Services no longer required. Just like that. Ah don't know. Work aw yer days an what've ye got tae show for it? Turn roon an kick ye in the teeth. Ah mean, what *have* ye got when ye come right down tae it.
15		Nothin.
	BILLY:	Ah might be able to get ye a start in our place. Cannae promise mind ye. An if there was anything it wouldnae be much. Maybe doin yer sweeper up or that.
	DAVIE:	Anythin's better than nothin.
	BILLY:	An once yer in the place, ye never know. Somethin better might come up.
20	DAVIE:	(*Dead*) Aye.
	BILLY:	Likes ae a storeman's job or that.
	DAVIE:	Aye.
	BILLY:	We never died a winter yet, eh?

(DAVIE *nods.* BILLY *exits*)

25	DAVIE:	Scrubbed. Get yer jacket on. Pick up yer cards. On yer way pal! Out the door.

(ALEC *is playing with yacht, positions fid like bowsprit, bow like mast, tries to make 'sail' with cellophane, can't hold all the separate bits, drops them.* DAVIE *comes in behind him*)

	DAVIE:	Bit of bad news son.

(*Pause*)

30		Ah've lost ma job. They gave me ma books.
	ALEC:	What'll we dae?
	DAVIE:	Billy says he might be able to fix me up wi something. Wouldnae be much. (*Shrugs*) Better than nothin. Ach, that was a lousy job anyway. Ah'm better off out ae it. Whatever happens. Place is a right mess eh. Amazin how it gets on top of ye.
35	ALEC:	Ah'll shove this in the Glory Hole. Out the road.

(*Folds up cellophane, puts tools in bag and picks up bow, yacht, carries the lot and exits*)

	DAVIE:	Ach aye. No to worry. Never died a winter yet.

| | | MARKS | STUDENT MARGIN |

Questions

1 Summarise what is said between Davie and Billy in lines 2–24. Make at least **four** key points.

MARKS: 4   **STUDENT MARGIN:** Understanding

> **Hint!**
>
> Question 1 is a **summarising** question. You are asked to make at least four key points. It is a good idea to bullet point your answer. In your answer you should explain, using your own words, what is said between Davie and Billy. There is no need to use quotations.

2 Explain how one example of sentence structure of lines 11–16 helps the audience to understand how Davie is feeling.

MARKS: 2   **STUDENT MARGIN:** Analysis

> **Hint!**
>
> Question 2 focuses on **sentence structure**. Therefore, you should only comment on this feature and show how it conveys Davie's feelings to the audience. You will need to make an appropriate reference to sentence structure and analyse how it shows Davie's feelings.

3 Explain how the dialogue in lines 18–25 emphasises the difference between Davie and Billy.

MARKS: 2   **STUDENT MARGIN:** Analysis

> **Hint!**
>
> Question 3 asks you to show your **understanding** of how Davie and Billy are different to one another. You will need to use your own words.

4 Explain what is revealed about **two** aspects of Davie's personality in lines 16–37.

MARKS: 4   **STUDENT MARGIN:** Analysis

> **Hint!**
>
> Question 4 asks you to comment in detail about what is revealed about Davie's personality in lines 16–37. This means that you will need to make appropriate references and comment on how they reveal Davie's personality to the audience.

5 By referring to the extract and to elsewhere in the play, show how the playwright presents the character of Davie.

MARKS: 8   **STUDENT MARGIN:** Evaluation

> **Hint!**
>
> Question 5 asks you to show how Alan Spence presents the character of Davie in this extract and the play as a whole. Up to 2 marks can be achieved for identifying elements of commonality as identified in the question. You can gain a further two marks by making a reference to the extract and commenting on how the playwright presents Davie. The final four marks are achieved by making reference to and analysing the presentation of Davie in the rest of the novel.

You can see example answers to these five questions in the Answers to Practice Questions section (page 25).

Prose

The Cone-Gatherers by Robin Jenkins

The extract is from Chapter 5. Calum and Neil are high in a tree; they hear Duror starting to climb towards them.

They heard the scrapes and thumps of his nailed boots on the rungs and then on the branches. A branch cracked suddenly. He exclaimed as if in anger, and paused for a full minute. When he resumed he climbed even more slowly than before. Soon he stopped again. He was still a long way below.

They waited, but he did not start to climb again. For three or four minutes they waited. Still he remained
5 motionless and silent. One of the dogs barked unhappily.

They thought he must have climbed as high as he wished, and now was admiring the view of the loch. After all, the tree was not private just because they happened to be in it; the ladder, too, belonged to the estate. At the same time Neil felt curiously embarrassed and could not think to start gathering cones again. Calum kept shivering.

10 They were far from guessing the truth, that Duror had ceased to climb because of fear; that, weak and dizzy and full of shame, he was clinging with ignominious tightness; that the dread of the descent was making him sick; and that he had almost forgotten his purpose in ascending to them.

At last Neil had to end the suspense.

'Hello, Mr. Duror,' he called. 'It's a grand day, isn't it?'

15 No reply came.

Neil tried again.

'Do you want to talk to us about something?' he shouted.

This time, after another long delay, there was a reply. They were surprised by the mildness of his voice. It was so faint too they had to strain to hear it.

20 'I've got a message for you,' he said.

'A message? Is it from Mr. Tulloch?'

There was a pause. 'Aye, from him.'

'Have we to go back home, to Ardmore?' cried Neil hopefully.

'You know these woods belong to Lady Runcie-Campbell?'

25 'We know that.'

'She wants you as beaters in a deer drive this afternoon.'

Neil was shocked.

'But we're here to gather cones,' he yelled. 'She can't order us about. She's not our mistress.'

'She telephoned Tulloch. He said you've to work for her this afternoon.'

30 'How could he? Didn't he tell us we'd to gather every cone we could? Didn't he ask us to work as much overtime as we liked? What's the good of all that if we're to be taken away for deer drives.' Neil's voice grew hoarse with indignation. 'My brother's never asked to take part in deer hunts,' he shouted. 'Mr. Tulloch knows that. I don't believe he knows anything about this. It's just a trick to get us to work for the lady.'

Duror was silent. His triumph was become a handful of withered leaves. When he had seen the ladder, he had
35 thought how gratifying it would be to deliver the deadly message to them in the eyrie where they fancied themselves safe. He had not anticipated this lightheadedness, this heaving of the stationary tree, this treachery of nature, this sickening of his very will to hate. He had never dreamed that he would not be able to do once only what the hunchback did several times a day. It seemed to him that he must therefore be far more ill and decayed than he had thought. He was like a tree still straight, still showing green leaves; but underground death
40 was creeping along the roots.

		MARKS	STUDENT MARGIN

2 Show how the poet's use of language in lines 13–18 conveys the way the relationship between the speaker and her husband has changed. Refer to **two** examples in your answer.

4   Understanding/analysis

> ⟩ *Hint!*
>
> Question 2 requires you to show your **understanding** of how the relationship between husband and wife has changed. You will need to make a reference to the text and comment on how the selection you have made conveys the change. It is likely that you will show what the relationship was like before and what it is like now. Again, this question is for four marks, therefore you need to do this twice.

3 By referring to **two** details in the speaker's dream (lines 19–24) explain how her fears are conveyed.

4   Understanding/analysis

> ⟩ *Hint!*
>
> Question 3 focuses on language, and asks you to **identify** and **explain**. You should explain how the speaker's fears are conveyed. You will need to make a reference to the text and comment on how the selection you have made conveys the speaker's fears. Again, this question is for four marks, therefore you need to do this twice.

4 By referring to this poem and to at least one other poem by Carol Ann Duffy, show how she explores tension within a relationship or within an individual.

8   Evaluation

> ⟩ *Hint!*
>
> Question 4 asks you to analyse how Duffy explores tension within a relationship or within an individual in this extract, and in at least one other poem by Duffy. You can gain up to two marks by identifying elements of commonality as identified in the question. You can gain a further two marks by making a reference to the extract and commenting on the tension. The final four marks are achieved by making reference to and analysing how aspects of tension within a relationship or within an individual are explored in other Duffy poems.

You can see example answers to these four questions in the Answers to Practice Questions section (page 27).

The Critical Essay

The Critical Essay is designed to test your skills in understanding, analysis and evaluation of the literature that you have studied as part of the course. Remember that you only write **one** Critical Essay and that it must come from a **different genre** to your Scottish Set Text. In each of the Critical Essay genres there will be two questions to choose from. There are 20 marks available and the examiner will take a holistic approach to deciding on a final mark.

Your response will be judged by your ability to demonstrate the following:

▶ Understanding
▶ Analysis
▶ Evaluation.

≫ HOW TO ANSWER

Understanding

The main way to show understanding is by demonstrating to the examiner that you are familiar with the text as a whole. In other words, you know what the text is about as well as having an understanding of its central concerns or themes. You must also show that you have an understanding of the question that you are answering.

Analysis

In your response you must show the examiner that you are aware of the writer's techniques and can use critical terminology to explain how particular stylistic features create effects and meaning for the reader. You will need to use appropriate references and quotations to support your answer.

Evaluation

In your essay you are demonstrating evaluation skills when you explain fully how effective the literary techniques employed by the writer are. You can do this by explaining in detail what you have enjoyed or what has been gained from the text, linking to and referring to a range of relevant features.

In summary, the examiner is looking for a response that is well written, well organised and relevant. You can do this by demonstrating a deep understanding of the text and the themes; showing knowledge and analysis of the literary techniques and features; and providing your own response and reaction to the text.

Choosing a question to answer

Choosing an appropriate question is key to being successful. In the exam hall you have a limited amount of time so you must settle on a question relatively quickly. Remember that you should go to the appropriate genre for your text and choose only one question. You will have two to choose from. The question you choose will be based on what you know about your text. This is why it is important to know your text thoroughly and have a high degree of familiarity. The different parts of the question will guide your response and ensure that your answer is relevant.

Let's look at this prose example.

Prose

> Answers to questions in this section should refer to the text and to such relevant features as: characterisation, setting, language, key incident(s), climax/turning point, plot, structure, narrative technique, theme, ideas, description …

1   Choose a novel or a short story or a work of non-fiction which has a memorable character/person, place or event.

By referring to appropriate techniques, explain how the writer makes the character/person, place or event memorable, and how this is important to the text as a whole.

As you can see, the question is in three parts. The first thing that you encounter before the questions is a text box. This is important as it points out the kind of features that you can focus on. This will help when you are planning your response.

The question itself provides you with a focus for your response. In this case you are asked to give an **explanation** of how the writer creates a memorable character/person, place or event and then **explain** how it is significant to the text as a whole.

By breaking down the question in this way, you will be absolutely clear on what the question is asking you to do. This will make the planning stage easier and, ultimately, means that you will write a response that is relevant. You may find it helpful to underline key words or phrases.

Planning your response

Planning your response is a good idea because it will provide a structure to your answer and also help stop you from rambling and going off task. In an exam situation you may feel the pressure of time, but spending some of that time on a plan will pay off in your response. It has already been stressed how important it is that your answer is relevant to the question you are answering. A plan will help you to do this. It doesn't need to be very detailed, but a series of six key bullet points or a mind-map will help you organise your ideas and can act as a memory aid or checklist. Although you will develop your own preferred way of planning, these points can be developed in your essay to become more extended paragraphs, and result in a coherent structure to your response.

Writing your response

Introduction

The introduction or opening paragraph of your essay is important as it highlights to the examiner that your essay is going to answer the question with points that are relevant. There are some vital pieces of information that should be included in the introduction:

► Title of the text you are writing about, and the name of the author.
► Some context as to what the text is about, making sure you refer to the central concerns or themes.
► A clear response to the question, which will set up your line of argument.
  The question will help you to do this.

Main paragraphs

Use your plan to organise your main paragraphs. This will give an overall structure to your essay. Each different point in your plan should be a new paragraph. The following approach to paragraph structure may help and can be remembered through the acronym P.E.A.R:

► Point – this is a obvious opening statement or point that makes it clear what the rest of the paragraph will be about.
► Evidence – this can come in the form of a direct quotation from the text or a reference from the text that supports your point.
► Analysis – this is when you explain in detail how the evidence you have given and literary techniques the writer uses answer the task. Your comments should be analytical and evaluative in nature.
► Reference back to question – link back to the focus of the task to ensure your answer is relevant.

The following words and phrases will help when it comes to analysing and evaluating the writer's techniques and style:

Analytical words (or alternatives to 'this shows')

- Conveys
- Depicts
- Embodies
- Emphasises
- Evokes
- Highlights
- Illuminates
- Implies
- Indicates
- Portrays
- Reinforces
- Reveals
- Suggests

For example:

- Here, the author indicates …
- By comparing … the writer suggests that …
- The image of … reinforces the idea that …

Top Tip!

Many students' essays can become unimaginative when it comes to the phrases they use for analysis and evaluation and they often rely heavily on the phrase 'this shows'. By using a variety of different phrases you will ensure that your response provides a well-developed commentary on the literary devices employed by the writer, as well as communicating your ideas in a way that is engaging to read.

Evaluative words

- Cleverly
- Creatively
- Disturbingly
- Effectively
- Emotively
- Evocatively
- Harrowingly
- Imaginatively
- Powerfully
- Realistically
- Skilfully
- Successfully

For example:

- This successfully portrays …
- The author powerfully conveys …
- The writer exploits setting effectively …

Linking expressions

You must ensure your paragraphs link together. This will help you develop a line of thought that is consistently relevant. You can do this by using a variety of linking expressions.

To show that you are adding to your argument you could use words and phrases such as:

- In addition
- Also
- Furthermore
- Besides
- Likewise
- Similarly
- In the same way
- Moreover

If you need to highlight a contrast, you could use words and phrases such as:

- Despite this
- However
- Yet
- Nevertheless
- On the other hand
- At the same time

If you need to show results, reasons and outcomes, you could use expressions such as:

- Therefore
- Hence
- Consequently
- Because of this
- For this reason
- In consequence
- Arising out of this

Conclusion

Your conclusion signals to the examiner that your response is coming to an end. Your conclusion should sum up the main points you have made. To indicate that you are about to conclude your argument, you should use phrases such as:

▶ In conclusion …
▶ In summary …
▶ To sum up …

You should refer to the key words of the question and the central concerns and themes of the text. You may also include a final overall evaluative comment on what you have enjoyed or gained from studying the text.

By the time of the actual exam you will have had plenty of practice and the questions contained at the end of this section and the Practice Papers will help you to be prepared.

The following questions are designed to give you opportunities to practise Critical Essay writing based on what you have read and studied. Remember that you cannot write on the same genre of your Scottish Set Text and you should only attempt **one** essay in the exam.

Drama

Answers to questions on Drama should refer to the text and to such relevant features as characterisation, key scene(s), structure, climax, theme, plot, conflict, setting …

1 Choose a play in which the playwright explores a theme that you feel is important.

   By referring to appropriate techniques, show how effectively the playwright establishes and explores the theme.

2 Choose a play which you feel has an effective opening scene or an effective final scene.

   By referring to appropriate techniques, explain why it is an effective way to start or to conclude the play as a whole.

Prose

Answers to questions on Prose should refer to the text and to such relevant features as characterisation, setting, language, key incident(s), climax, turning point, plot, structure, narrative technique, theme, ideas, description …

3 Choose a novel **or** a short story in which a character is in conflict with another character or with a group of characters or with society as a whole.

   By referring to appropriate techniques, show how the conflict arises and what effect it has on the character's fate in the novel or short story as a whole.

4 Choose a novel **or** short story **or** work of non-fiction which has a key incident or a turning point.

   By referring to appropriate techniques, show how this incident is important to the text as a whole.

Poetry

Answers to questions on Poetry should refer to the text and to such relevant features as word choice, tone, imagery, structure, content, rhythm, rhyme, theme, sound, ideas …

5 Choose a poem which made a deep impression on you.

   By referring to poetic techniques, show how the poet made this deep impression.

6 Choose a poem which portrays an interesting character.

   By referring to poetic techniques, show how the poet makes the character interesting.

Film and Television Drama

Answers to questions on Film and Television Drama should refer to the text and to such relevant features as use of camera, key sequence, characterisation, mise-en-scène, editing, setting, music/sound, special effects, plot, dialogue …

7   Choose a scene **or** sequence from a film or television drama which you think is sad or exciting or moving or funny or frightening.

By referring to appropriate techniques, explain how the director leads you to feel this way.

Hint!

'Television drama' includes a single play, a series or a serial.

8   Choose a film or television drama which has a memorable main character.

By referring to appropriate techniques, explain how the character is presented in the film or television drama as a whole.

Language

Answers to questions on Language should refer to the text and to such relevant features as register, accent, dialect, slang, jargon, vocabulary, tone, abbreviation …

9   Choose **two** advertisements which aim to persuade you to change your opinion or to buy something or to change your behaviour.

By referring to specific examples, explain how successful the persuasive language is.

10 Consider the ways that young people use the internet to communicate and socialise, for example social networking sites or instant messaging or chat rooms or blogs.

By referring to specific examples and to appropriate techniques, explain how these communications differ from standard English and what their attractions are for young people.

Hint!

→   Familiarise yourself with the main ideas/themes/message in your class text(s)
→   Make sure you know key details of texts for your introduction – title, writer, genre of text, context, themes/key ideas/message
→   Revise key analytical techniques and points
→   Create revision notes, e.g. mind-maps or lists around the key features such as characterisation, setting, language, key incident(s), climax, turning point, plot, structure, theme, ideas, description, poetic techniques
→   Identify and learn a range of quotations which are evidence of key ideas/techniques
→   Practise introducing, integrating and analysing these quotations
→   Practise writing example introductions/conclusions
→   Practise essay planning based around a specific task (the questions and Practice Papers in this book will help).

Stop our oceans choking on a plastic overdose

Question	Answer text	Marks available	Additional guidance/possible answers
1	You should explain in your own words why plastic pollution has become a global concern. Each key point (1) × 3	3	▸ plastic contamination is increasing ▸ animals that live in the sea are becoming endangered ▸ plastics are also a threat to people
2	You should summarise, in your own words, the action that we need to take to reduce plastic use. Each key point (1) × 5	5	▸ limit the amount of plastic we use ▸ impose charges for items made out of plastic ▸ reduce plastic packaging in products ▸ manufacturers could make it easier to recycle by labelling products clearly ▸ invent better ways of dealing with plastic
3	You should explain how the language used makes it clear that action against plastic pollution is needed. Reference (1) plus appropriate comment (1) × 2	4	▸ '(political) concern' (1) shows that the government is worried about plastic pollution (1) ▸ 'toxic time bomb' (1) shows that just as a bomb causes devastation and destruction so too can plastic pollution become a critical situation if not addressed (1) ▸ positioning of 'Rarely' at start (1) to emphasise how important an issue this is for society (1) ▸ 'aroused' (1) suggests that plastic pollution has provoked public debate ▸ 'lethal debris' (1) suggests that plastic pollution has the ability to cause deaths (1) ▸ 'alarm' (1) suggests that plastic pollution can cause fear and panic (1)
4	You must comment on two different language features used to explain how the writer makes clear the extent of plastic pollution. Reference (1) plus appropriate comment (1) × 2	4	▸ 'small fraction of the trillions of plastic pieces'. (1) The use of contrast shows how only a very tiny amount of plastic can be taken out of the seas compared with the huge number of plastic items (1) ▸ 'plastic bottles, charges for plastic bags and coffee cups, and bans on certain products, such as the one proposed last week by Theresa May, UK prime minister, on plastic straws and cotton buds' (1) use of a list shows the variety and quantity of plastic products that cause pollution and the charge is a possible solution that the government is putting forward (1) ▸ 'floating debris' (1) suggests rubbish (1) ▸ 'notorious Great Pacific Garbage Patch' (1) suggests that the area is infamous for its rubbish (1) ▸ 'unrealistic' (1) suggests that the challenge is too great (1) ▸ 'rapidly reducing' (1) suggests that plastic use must decrease quickly (1) ▸ 'unnecessary plastic packaging' (1) suggests that wrapping is excessive (1)

Film and Television Drama

Answers to questions on Film and Television Drama should refer to the text and to such relevant features as use of camera, key sequence, characterisation, mise-en-scène, editing, setting, music/sound, special effects, plot, dialogue …

7   Choose a scene **or** sequence from a film or television drama which you think is sad or exciting or moving or funny or frightening.

By referring to appropriate techniques, explain how the director leads you to feel this way.

8   Choose a film or television drama which has a memorable main character.

By referring to appropriate techniques, explain how the character is presented in the film or television drama as a whole.

> **Hint!**
> 'Television drama' includes a single play, a series or a serial.

Language

Answers to questions on Language should refer to the text and to such relevant features as register, accent, dialect, slang, jargon, vocabulary, tone, abbreviation …

9   Choose **two** advertisements which aim to persuade you to change your opinion or to buy something or to change your behaviour.

By referring to specific examples, explain how successful the persuasive language is.

10 Consider the ways that young people use the internet to communicate and socialise, for example social networking sites or instant messaging or chat rooms or blogs.

By referring to specific examples and to appropriate techniques, explain how these communications differ from standard English and what their attractions are for young people.

> **Hint!**
> → Familiarise yourself with the main ideas/themes/message in your class text(s)
> → Make sure you know key details of texts for your introduction – title, writer, genre of text, context, themes/key ideas/message
> → Revise key analytical techniques and points
> → Create revision notes, e.g. mind-maps or lists around the key features such as characterisation, setting, language, key incident(s), climax, turning point, plot, structure, theme, ideas, description, poetic techniques
> → Identify and learn a range of quotations which are evidence of key ideas/techniques
> → Practise introducing, integrating and analysing these quotations
> → Practise writing example introductions/conclusions
> → Practise essay planning based around a specific task (the questions and Practice Papers in this book will help).

Reading for Understanding, Analysis and Evaluation

Why didn't people smile in old photos?

Question	Answer text	Marks available	Additional guidance/possible answers
1	You should explain in your own words two key points the writer is making about early photographic portraits. Each key point (1) × 2	2	▶ the people in them are not smiling (1) ▶ they all look very stern/grave/dejected/miserable (1)
2	You should summarise, using your own words as far as possible, the evidence the writer gives that 'People in the past were not necessarily more gloomy than we are'. Any five of the points in the 'Additional guidance' column for 5 marks. Be aware of and use condensed answers.	5	Glosses of: ▶ 'did not go around in a perpetual state of sorrow', e.g. they weren't by nature gloomy all the time (1) ▶ 'they might be forgiven for doing so', e.g. although they had good reason not to be happy (1) because of … ▶ … 'higher mortality rates … medicine that was puny', e.g. likely to die young (1) ▶ 'had a sense of humour even about the darkest aspects of their society', e.g. they could laugh at even rather grim things (1) ▶ joking reference to cholera in *Three Men in a Boat* (1) ▶ Chaucer still funny despite being written at time of plague (1) ▶ Jane Austen makes witty comments during period of war (1) ▶ 'Laughter and jollity … institutionalised', e.g. enjoyment/fun were built into the way of life (1) ▶ celebration of Christmas as a time of fun is contemporary with the invention of photography (1)
3	You should explain how two examples of the writer's word choice demonstrate his liking for old photographs. Reference (1) plus appropriate comment (1) × 2	4	▶ 'introspection' (1) suggests the people in them are deep thinkers (1) ▶ 'haunt' (1) suggests there is something mysteriously enticing, alluring about them (1) ▶ 'seriousness' (1) suggests they are important, weighty, not trivial (1) ▶ '(more) moving' (1) suggests they affect him emotionally (1) ▶ 'grandeur' (1) suggests splendour, magnificence (1) ▶ 'gravitas' (1) suggests seriousness, solemnity (1) ▶ 'traditional' (1) suggests established, worth keeping, to be admired (1)

Question	Answer text	Marks available	Additional guidance/possible answers
4	You should explain how two examples of the language used demonstrate his dislike of modern photography. Reference (1) plus appropriate comment (1) × 2	4	▸ positioning of 'Today' at start (1) emphasises intention to compare unfavourable attitude to modern photography with his liking of old photographs (1) ▸ sound effect in 'so many smiling snaps' (1) creates slightly humorous, sarcastic tone (1) ▸ 'snaps' (1) sounds unimportant, trivial (compared with 'portraiture') (1) ▸ 'absurd' (1) suggests that looking for anything worthwhile in these photos is stupid (1) ▸ series of short sentences (from 'Photos …' onwards) (1) suggests how simple, uncomplicated these ideas are (1) ▸ 'smile, laugh and cavort' (1) list of behaviours shows how much stupidity is involved (1) ▸ repetition of 'endless/endlessly' (1) emphasises how tedious this behaviour is (1) ▸ use of slang 'selfie' (1) suggests contempt for the whole idea (1) ▸ 'momentary' (1) suggests it is fleeting, unsubstantial, insincere (1) ▸ 'performance' (1) suggests it's an act (1) ▸ repetition of 'zero' (1) emphasises how meaningless it is (1) ▸ 'disturbingly' (1) suggests he finds it rather alarming, unnerving (1) ▸ 'throwaway' (1) emphasises its transience, lack of substance (1) ▸ use of parenthesis (1) adds a light-hearted remark to make them sound even worse (1) ▸ simplicity of 'just press delete' (1) emphasises how disposable these photographs are (1)
5	You should explain how the opening paragraph is an effective introduction. Each key point (1) × 2	2	▸ the writer addresses the reader directly by using 'you' (1) ▸ the use of the second person pronoun involves the reader, which makes you want to continue reading (1)
6	You should explain why the last paragraph provides an effective conclusion to the passage as a whole. Any two of the points in the 'Additional guidance' column for 2 marks.	2	▸ continues praise of old photographs (1) ▸ 'beautiful and haunting' makes them sound particularly appealing (1) ▸ continues to be dismissive of modern photographs (1) ▸ 'silly selfies' is particularly scathing (1) ▸ repeats idea that in the past there was as much fun, enjoyment as today (1) ▸ presents older subjects as more dignified ('no hysterical need') (1) ▸ repeats idea that the subjects had serious thoughts on their minds (1) ▸ sums up with clear comparison/contrast: 'grave realities'; 'inanely happy … snaps' (1)

Stop our oceans choking on a plastic overdose

Question	Answer text	Marks available	Additional guidance/possible answers
1	You should explain in your own words why plastic pollution has become a global concern. Each key point (1) × 3	3	▸ plastic contamination is increasing ▸ animals that live in the sea are becoming endangered ▸ plastics are also a threat to people
2	You should summarise, in your own words, the action that we need to take to reduce plastic use. Each key point (1) × 5	5	▸ limit the amount of plastic we use ▸ impose charges for items made out of plastic ▸ reduce plastic packaging in products ▸ manufacturers could make it easier to recycle by labelling products clearly ▸ invent better ways of dealing with plastic
3	You should explain how the language used makes it clear that action against plastic pollution is needed. Reference (1) plus appropriate comment (1) × 2	4	▸ '(political) concern' (1) shows that the government is worried about plastic pollution (1) ▸ 'toxic time bomb' (1) shows that just as a bomb causes devastation and destruction so too can plastic pollution become a critical situation if not addressed (1) ▸ positioning of 'Rarely' at start (1) to emphasise how important an issue this is for society (1) ▸ 'aroused' (1) suggests that plastic pollution has provoked public debate ▸ 'lethal debris' (1) suggests that plastic pollution has the ability to cause deaths (1) ▸ 'alarm' (1) suggests that plastic pollution can cause fear and panic (1)
4	You must comment on two different language features used to explain how the writer makes clear the extent of plastic pollution. Reference (1) plus appropriate comment (1) × 2	4	▸ 'small fraction of the trillions of plastic pieces'. (1) The use of contrast shows how only a very tiny amount of plastic can be taken out of the seas compared with the huge number of plastic items (1) ▸ 'plastic bottles, charges for plastic bags and coffee cups, and bans on certain products, such as the one proposed last week by Theresa May, UK prime minister, on plastic straws and cotton buds' (1) use of a list shows the variety and quantity of plastic products that cause pollution and the charge is a possible solution that the government is putting forward (1) ▸ 'floating debris' (1) suggests rubbish (1) ▸ 'notorious Great Pacific Garbage Patch' (1) suggests that the area is infamous for its rubbish (1) ▸ 'unrealistic' (1) suggests that the challenge is too great (1) ▸ 'rapidly reducing' (1) suggests that plastic use must decrease quickly (1) ▸ 'unnecessary plastic packaging' (1) suggests that wrapping is excessive (1)

Question	Answer text	Marks available	Additional guidance/possible answers
5	You must explain how the opening paragraph is an effective introduction. Reference (1) plus appropriate comment (1)	2	▸ 'may pose a toxic time bomb for marine life and eventually humans too' (1) ▸ The use of emotive imagery is effective in capturing the reader's attention and highlights that plastic pollution is not just an issue for sea creatures but also is a potential threat to people too. The dramatic opening makes the reader want to read more (1)
6	You must select an appropriate expression and explain how it contributes to an effective conclusion. Reference (1) plus appropriate comment (1)	2	▸ 'action is needed urgently' (1) returns to the opening 'more rapidly than plastic pollution' ▸ 'The battle against unnecessary plastics will not be so straightforward' (1) returns to the idea of 'a grand challenge'/'global scale' (1) ▸ The use of the comparison between CFCs and plastic (1) is effective as a conclusion because it highlights how, like plastics, CFCs were a serious issue and a solution was found. (1)

Critical Reading

Sailmaker by Alan Spence

Question	Answer text	Marks available	Additional guidance/possible answers
1	You must summarise what is in lines 2–24 and make at least four key points. Each key point (1) × 4	4	▸ Davie tells Billy he has lost his job (1) ▸ Billy says it's not Davie's fault/not fair/criticises employers (1) ▸ Davie is very defeatist/thinks he's got nothing going for him (1) ▸ Billy says he might be able to get him a job (1) ▸ Davie displays little enthusiasm (1) ▸ Billy tries to keep Davie's spirits up (1)
2	You must explain how the sentence structure of lines 11–16 helps the audience to understand how Davie is feeling. Reference (1) plus appropriate comment (1)	2	▸ exclamation (1) shows his feeling of hopelessness, defeat (1) ▸ use of italics (1) shows how resentful he feels about 'them' (1) ▸ series of short sentences (1) suggests he is disengaged, depressed, has given up (1) ▸ series of questions (1) suggests he is at a loss, feels hopeless (1)
3	You must explain how the dialogue in lines 18–25 emphasises the difference between Davie and Billy. Reference (1) plus appropriate comment (1)	2	▸ Davie has very little to say/is monosyllabic/sounds defeated (1) ▸ Billy talks at greater length/offers hope/encouragement (1)

Question	Answer text	Marks available	Additional guidance/possible answers
4	You must explain what is revealed about two aspects of Davie's personality in lines 15–37. Reference (1) plus appropriate comment (1) × 2	4	▶ unambitious/never one to get excited (1) 'wouldnae be much' (1) ▶ feels sort of powerless to affect anything (1) '*Shrugs*' (1) ▶ takes life as it comes (1) 'better than nothin' (1) ▶ keen to rationalise/make best of situation (1) 'that was a lousy job anyway' (1) ▶ mild surprise at something trivial (1) 'Amazin how it gets on top of ye' (1) ▶ resigned acceptance of everything (1) 'Ach aye. No to worry.' (1) ▶ clichéd optimism (or possible ironic repetition of Billy earlier) (1) 'Never died a winter yet' (1)
5	You must, by referring to the extract and to elsewhere in the play, show how the playwright presents the character of Davie. Identify the commonality (2). Reference and comment about Davie's character from the extract (2). Make reference to and analyse aspects of Davie's character from elsewhere in the play (4).	8	Aspects of Davie's character that are worthy of comment include: ▶ his self-pitying nature ▶ his lack of drive and/or ambition ▶ he takes refuge in drink ▶ he loves his son but doesn't really understand him ▶ he lives in the past ▶ he always hopes that things will improve, but is never very confident ▶ he is passive and just lets life happen to him.

The Cone-Gatherers by Robin Jenkins

Question	Answer text	Marks available	Additional guidance/possible answers
1	You must summarise what happens in this extract from the novel in your own words. Each key point (1) × 4	4	▶ Duror is unable to climb the tree (1) ▶ Neil is initially polite (1) ▶ Duror delivers the message to Calum and Neil about the deer drive (1) ▶ Neil protests strongly (1) ▶ the effect on Duror of being unable to climb the tree is evident (1)
2	You must give one example to show how the writer creates a tense mood in the first two paragraphs. Reference (1) plus appropriate comment (1)	2	▶ 'scrapes'/'thumps'/'cracked'/'barked' (1) use of onomatopoeia to create threatening sounds (1) ▶ the frequency of short sentences (1) creates a breathless, staccato effect (1) ▶ the alternation between sound and silence (1) creates suspense (1) ▶ he references waiting, once for 'three or four minutes' (1) an agonisingly long time (1) ▶ the barking of the dog (1) could be seen as intimidating (1)

Question	Answer text	Marks available	Additional guidance/possible answers
3	You must show how Neil's attitude towards Duror goes through at least two changes. Reference (1) plus appropriate comment (1) × 2	4	▸ is initially friendly/polite ('It's a grand day, isn't it?') (1) ▸ tries to be helpful ('Do you want to talk to us about something?') (1) ▸ sees Duror as possible bringer of good news ('Have we to go back home?') (1) ▸ is non-committal/defensive ('We know that.') (1) ▸ is angry/slightly aggressive ('How could he?'/repeated 'Didn't he …') (1) ▸ is disbelieving/indignant ('What's the good of all that …') (1) ▸ becomes very assertive ('It's just a trick') (1)
4	You must explain what the image in the last sentence of the extract tells the reader about Duror. Reference (1) plus appropriate comment (1)	2	▸ on the outside he appears normal/healthy (1) but a malignant force is destroying him from within (1) ▸ on the outside he looks strong (1) but there is a hidden decay beneath (1)
5	You must, by referring to the extract and to elsewhere in the novel, show how the conflict between Duror and the cone-gatherers is explored. Identify the commonality (2). Reference and comment on Duror and the cone-gatherers' conflict from the extract (2). Making reference to and analysing aspects of the conflict between Duror and the cone-gatherers elsewhere in the play (4).	8	▸ Duror's hatred for them from the outset ▸ the irrational nature of Duror's hatred ▸ Duror's silent vigil at their hut ▸ the deer drive ▸ Duror's lies and attempts to blacken their reputation ▸ the incident in the pub ▸ the climax of the novel

Mrs Midas by Carol Ann Duffy

Question	Answer text	Marks available	Additional guidance/possible answers
1	You must refer to two examples and show how the poet creates a light-hearted, humorous tone. Each key point (1) × 4	4	▸ 'keep his hands to himself' (1) normally a criticism of someone making unwanted advances, but here emphasising the need for him not to touch anything (lest it turn to gold) (1) ▸ 'The toilet I didn't mind' (1) having taken precautions with the cat and the phone, she appears not to mind the prospect of sitting on a gold toilet (1) ▸ '… we all have wishes; granted./But who has wishes granted?' (1) wordplay involving two takes on 'wishes granted' (1. = I accept that everyone makes wishes; 2. = nobody actually has them come true) (1) ▸ 'you'll be able to give up smoking for good' (1) the fact that he is unable to light a cigarette (because it turns to gold) leads her to joke that now he'll (finally) be able to stop smoking (1)

Question	Answer text	Marks available	Additional guidance/possible answers
2	You must give two examples to explain how the language conveys the way the relationship between the speaker and husband has changed. Reference (1) plus appropriate comment (1) × 2	4	Now: ▸ 'Separate beds' (1) minor sentence to suggest the simplicity (inevitability) of the change to less intimacy (1) ▸ 'put a chair against my door' (1) suggests fear, need for protection (1) ▸ 'near petrified' (1) suggests state of heightened fear (1) ▸ 'turning the spare room/into the tomb of Tutankhamun' (1) slightly jokey reference suggests an element of contempt (1) ▸ 'feared his honeyed embrace' (1) suggests she is frightened of him, of the possible effect on her (1) ▸ 'turn my lips to a work of art' (1) suggests that something alive, capable of showing love, will become something inanimate (1) Before: ▸ 'passionate' (1) suggests loving, fervent relationship (1) ▸ 'halcyon days' (1) suggests a glorious, heavenly, untroubled time (1) ▸ 'unwrapping each other' (1) suggests sensual, loving, intimate process (1) ▸ 'rapidly' (1) suggests uncontrolled desire (1) ▸ 'like presents' (1) suggests generosity, reciprocal love, warmth, happiness (1) ▸ 'fast food' (1) suggests simple, guilty pleasure (1)
3	You must give two details from the speaker's dream and explain how her fears are conveyed. Reference (1) plus appropriate comment (1) × 2	4	▸ 'its perfect ore limbs' (1) suggests the baby's arms/legs are inanimate, lifeless (1) ▸ 'tongue/like a precious latch' (1) suggests tongue (connotations of speech/kissing) is inanimate, concerned with fastening, obstructing entry (1) ▸ 'amber eyes/holding their pupils like flies' (1) suggests lifelessness, distortion of the human, restriction of key sense of sight (1) ▸ 'dream-milk/burned in my breasts' (1) suggests pain, thwarting of maternal of love (1)
4	You must, by referring to the extract and to at least one other poem by Duffy, show how she explores tension within a relationship or within an individual. Identify the commonality (2). Reference and comment on tensions within the relationship in the extract (2). Make reference to and analyse tensions within relationships or within an individual in at least one other poem by Duffy (4).	8	▸ *Mrs Midas*: tension within relationship with husband; tension in her own mind at the end: she misses him physically ▸ *The Way My Mother Speaks*: tension within speaker during journey, feels caught between two worlds, finds reassurance in memories of mother's speech patterns ▸ *In Mrs Tilscher's Class*: tension between safe world of the classroom and external horrors of Brady and Hindley; tension between speaker and some classmates; tension within speaker at onset of puberty ▸ *Originally*: tension within the family (brothers' complaints and parents' anxiety); tension within herself over 'where she comes from' ▸ *War Photographer*: tension between photographer and the newspaper readers; tension in his own mind about the nature of the images he captures ▸ *Valentine*: relationships seen as poisonous/dangerous, doomed to fail; tension between the conventional and the unconventional

Reading for Understanding, Analysis and Evaluation

> **Duration: 1 hour**
> **Total marks: 30**
> **Attempt ALL questions.**
> Write your answers clearly in the answer booklet provided. In the answer booklet you must clearly identify the question number you are attempting.
> Use **blue** or **black** ink.
> Before leaving the examination room you must give your answer booklet to the Invigilator; if you do not, you may lose all the marks for this paper.

Sport will continue to transcend the ages

At the weekend, I watched a fair bit of sport. I watched the cricket on Sky Sports Ashes, the Manchester United v Tottenham Hotspur game on Sky Sports 1, Match of the Day on BBC One, a bit of the Football League Tonight show on Channel 5 and the headlines on Sky Sports News at Ten. I could also have watched Sky Sports F1; BT Sport 1 and 2; Eurosport 1 and 2; MUTV, Chelsea TV, Premier Sports, Racing UK, BoxNation, and dozens of other
5 digital channels devoted to live, recorded and highlighted sport.

The pre-eminent position of sport in our media-dominated culture is well established. But it is worth taking a step back to see just how unexpected this development has been. It is remarkable to note that not a single English top-flight football match was broadcast before Christmas in the 1985–86 season, owing to a dispute between the FA and TV stations. There was only a small outcry from the public. Today, there might have been rioting.

10 If you rewind just a little farther back, the cultural significance of sport today seems even more striking. In the middle of the 19th century, the Olympic Games didn't exist and neither did the World Cup. There were almost no governing bodies.

As for most of the previous 15 centuries, sport was a fringe activity out of keeping with religious sensibilities, which regarded kicking and hitting balls as a frivolous pastime. The bulk of individuals in the western world
15 went through life without any conception that these invented games would one day come to dominate global consciousness.

When I was in my teens, it wasn't just the history of sport that looked bleak, the future did as well. When I went to a careers evening at school and said that I wanted to become a sports journalist, the adviser spluttered. She doubted that sport would be big enough to support such a career. She pointed to the growth in technology,
20 video games, virtual reality and a host of other things that were set to transform leisure time. 'I doubt many people will be watching sport 20 years from now,' she said.

This wasn't just her view, it was the consensus among many social commentators. The idea that sport might soon become dominant and pre-eminent in the media would have been laughed at. That is why the trajectory of sport's growth is worth reflecting upon.

25 It is not only represented in the proliferation of TV channels, it is also stimulating this proliferation. 'Premium sports content' drives subscriptions. The jostle between BT and Sky over football rights (reaching fever pitch in advertising spend at present) is where the war over broadband may be won and lost.

The possibility that Google, Netflix and the like will start to bid for premium sports rights is predicated upon the same logic. These corporate giants know that if they wish to build new markets (and cut the legs from under
30 traditional players, such as Sky), they have to use sport as a Trojan horse. In a world where sport is the dominant feature of social interaction, there is no other way.

There has been a proliferation in radio stations (such as TalkSPORT, Radio 5 live and sports extra) too, along with hundreds of podcasts and blogs. Far from being replaced by new technologies, as my careers adviser predicted, sport has colonised them. Football is the most prevalent theme on Twitter. And it is what people want to watch
35 on a growing list of devices, whether tablets, laptops or, increasingly, the latest generation of smartphones.

Simultaneously, the social function of sport is solidifying. It is the chosen vehicle to break the ice when we (particularly men) talk to each other, whether at an office meeting or wherever else. It is pretty much the only activity that allows large sections of society to come together in a shared experience, such as when your home country is playing a World Cup match.

40 How did this astonishing transformation in the meaning of sport come about? Perhaps the crucial turning point came with the project to redefine sport's moral status in the Victorian era. The idea that games such as rugby, football and cricket help young people to respect rules and develop character created an impetus to codify games and establish functioning governing bodies, which spread throughout the empire.

But where next? When I started in sports journalism, I wondered if the bubble would soon burst. I looked for a
45 tipping point, subtle signs that the infatuation was petering out. Today, however, I suspect that sport is here to stay as a cultural giant. This is not a bubble, it is something more permanent. Instead of interpreting the past century and a half as an aberration, it is possible to see the centuries beforehand as the true anomaly.

When you take the long view, the present status of sport seems entirely natural. Consider that the Ancient Olympics, the most significant human festival of antiquity, lasted, without interruption, for 1,170 years. This
50 longevity has no precedent. The festival, to which spectators flocked from throughout the Greek world, was not interrupted by pestilence, by war, and certainly not by apathy.

This suggests that sport will sustain its present standing because, as with the ancient festivals, it speaks to something permanent in the human psyche. No amount of technological, economic, religious or social change will eradicate this, except temporarily, as in the medieval period. These unscripted sporting dramas move and
55 inspire us. They evoke themes of competition, teamwork and rivalry, which are central to the human condition. They help people to escape the humdrum and ordinary.

Sport is here to stay.

Matthew Syed, in *The Times*

		MARKS
1	Explain fully why the first paragraph (lines 1–5) is an effective opening to the passage as a whole.	2
2	Look at lines 6–16. Explain **in your own words four** ways in which the importance of sport has changed over the years.	4
3	Look at lines 17–21. Explain what the careers adviser's attitude was to sports journalism, and how one example of the writer's **word choice** makes this attitude clear.	3
4	Look at lines 25–31. Explain how **two** examples of the writer's **word choice** demonstrate how fierce the competition is among TV channels.	4
5	Look at lines 33–39. Explain using **your own words** as far as possible **five** pieces of evidence the writer gives to show that the careers adviser was wrong about people's interest in sport.	5
6	Look at lines 40–43. Explain **in your own words** the importance of the 'Victorian era' in changing attitudes to sport. You should make **two** key points in your answer.	2
7	Look at lines 44–47. Explain how two examples of the language used (such as **word choice**, **sentence structure** or **imagery**) demonstrate the writer's feelings about sport.	4
8	Look at lines 48–51. Explain **in your own words** three reasons why the writer refers to the Ancient Olympics to support his argument.	3
9	Look at lines 52–56. Explain **in your own words** three reasons why, according to the writer, sport is important to us.	3

[End of question paper]

Critical Reading

Duration: 90 minutes
Total marks: 40

SECTION 1 – Scottish Text – 20 marks

Read an extract from a Scottish text you have previously studied.

Choose ONE text from either

Part A – Drama

or

Part B – Prose

or

Part C – Poetry

Attempt ALL the questions for your chosen text.

SECTION 2 – Critical Essay – 20 marks

Attempt ONE question from the following genres – Drama, Prose, Poetry, Film and Television Drama, or Language.

Your answer must be on a different genre from that chosen in Section 1.

You should spend approximately 45 minutes on each Section.

Write your answers clearly in the answer booklet provided. In the answer booklet you must clearly identify the question number you are attempting.

Use **blue** or **black** ink.

Before leaving the examination room you must give your answer booklet to the Invigilator; if you do not, you may lose all the marks for this paper.

Section 1 – Scottish Text – 20 marks

Part A – Scottish Text – Drama

Text 1 – Drama

If you choose this text you may not attempt a question on Drama in Section 2.

Read the extract below and then attempt the following questions.

Bold Girls *by Rona Munro*

The extract is from Scene One. The women recall the night Cassie's husband was arrested.

NORA:	Oh do you remember the night they took Joe? You should've seen me, Marie.
CASSIE:	She was something that night, Andytown's own Incredible Hulk, 'Don't get me angry'!
NORA:	Well Marie, there was wee Cassie —
CASSIE:	Wee? I'm wee again am I?
5 NORA:	—just a week out the hospital with the stitches still in from the section that gave us Teresa, and I open my door and here she is running up the road —
CASSIE:	That was when we had our own house, you know, at the end there —
NORA:	Squealing 'Mummy! Mummy!' —
CASSIE:	—one hand clutching my stomach 'cause I'm sure the whole lot's going to fall out.
0 NORA:	—'Mummy! Mummy! They're taking Joe!' Well I just felt my blood rise —
CASSIE:	She was a lioness. She was.
NORA:	—I marched back up the road and here they were, dragging the poor man out of his own house without even a pair of shoes on his feet —

	CASSIE:	He'd been snoring away in front of the football, toasting his toes, with a pie in one hand and a can in the other.
15		
	NORA:	Sure he'd not been ready for any trouble; why would he be?
	CASSIE:	And the rest of them are throwing everything every which way and all over the house and the baby's screaming and the child's calling for her daddy —
20	NORA:	And he keeps his hand tight round this pie the whole time they were dragging him away. And I goes up to this big RUC man and I says —
	CASSIE:	She picked the biggest.
	NORA:	I says, 'What's the charges? Where's your warrants?'
	CASSIE:	And he's peering down at her like he's a mountain and she's a beetle at the bottom of it.
	NORA:	And he says 'And who are you?' And I says, 'I'm that boy's mother-in-law, and before you take
25		him you'll have to answer to me!'
	CASSIE:	Can you beat it, Marie?
	NORA:	And he says, 'You get out of our way Mrs or it'll be the worse for you.'
	CASSIE:	He didn't say it as nice as that Mummy, there was a few fucking old …
	NORA:	We do not need to use language like that Cassie! 'Out the way or it'll be the worse for you,'
30		he says. Oh he was a big bastard Marie. 'Oh,' I says, 'Oh would you strike a woman that could be your own mother? Would you now?' (*She starts to laugh*)
	MARIE:	What happened?
	CASSIE:	Wallop! Knocked her straight through the hedge.
	NORA:	(*still laughing*) Would you hit a mother? Sure I got my answer on the end of his fist.
35	CASSIE:	Nearly choked on her false teeth.
	NORA:	I did.
	CASSIE:	I didn't know which of them to go to first, Joe, or Mummy in the hedge with her little legs waving in the air.
	NORA:	(*wiping her eyes, still laughing*) Oh – oh but that was a terrible night.

MARKS

1 **a)** Look at lines 1–11.
Referring closely to two examples from these lines, show how Cassie's admiration for Nora is conveyed.

4

b) Explain how the dramatist conveys the liveliness of the dialogue in these lines.

2

2 Explain **one** way in which the language of lines 12–18 conveys how fast-moving the incident was.

2

3 Look at lines 19–38. Explain how the dramatist creates humour in the way Cassie and Nora recall the event.
You should refer to **two** examples in your answer.

4

4 By referring to the extract and to elsewhere in the play, show how the women's lives are affected by 'The Troubles'.

8

Text 2 – Drama

If you choose this text you may not attempt a question on Drama in Section 2.

Read the extract below and then attempt the following questions.

Sailmaker *by Alan Spence*

The extract is from Act Two. Davie arrives home from the pub.

DAVIE:	(*Noticing* ALEC) Yawright son?
ALEC:	(*Not looking up*) Aye.
DAVIE:	Ach aye. Yirra good boy. What ye readin?
ALEC:	A book.
5 DAVIE:	Naw! Whit book!
ALEC:	David Copperfield. Got an exam next week.
DAVIE:	Dickens, eh? Now yer talkin. Ah've read aw his books. The lot. Got them all out the library. Used tae read a lot ye know. Dickens is the greatest. David Copperfield is it?
ALEC:	That's what ah said.
10 DAVIE:	Mr Micawber. Somethin'll turn up, eh?
	Income twenty pounds, expenditure nineteen pounds nineteen and six: result happiness.
	Income twenty pounds, expenditure twenty pounds and sixpence: result …
	(*Shrugs*)
	Not to worry.
15	Hey, ah got ye crisps. Bottle ae Irn Bru. (*Puts them on table*)
ALEC:	(*Grudging*) Thanks.
DAVIE:	Any chance ae a cuppa tea?
ALEC:	There's some left in the pot. (DAVIE *pours dregs*)
DAVIE:	(*Sings*)
20	Where the blue of the night
	Meets the gold of the day
	(*To* ALEC) Cheer up. (*No response*) C'mon. (*Spars*)
ALEC:	Chuck it will ye!
DAVIE:	Torn face.
25 ALEC:	Ah didnae know where ye wur.
DAVIE:	Och …
ALEC:	Might have been under a bus or anythin.
DAVIE:	(*Sighs*) Look. Ah'm sorry, awright? Just … wan a these things, ye know.
ALEC:	Aye ah know.
30 DAVIE:	Good company. Nae harm in it. Didnae even have a lot tae drink. It's just good tae relax.
	Wee refreshment. Ach aye. The patter was good tae.
	Kenny's a great Burns man. Could recite Tam O'Shanter tae ye just like that! Yer sittin talkin away and he'll come out wi a line fae it.
	Fast by an ingle, bleezing finely
35	Wi reamin swats that drank divinely
	Great stuff eh? Poetry!
	Reamin swats!
	Anythin for eatin?
ALEC:	Naw.
40 DAVIE:	Nothin?
ALEC:	Not a thing.
DAVIE:	What about that tin a soup?

ALEC:	Ah had it for ma tea.	
DAVIE:	Oh aye. An the creamed rice?	
45 ALEC:	Ah ate that tae.	
DAVIE:	Themorra ah'll get a nice bit steak. Have it wi chips. Fried tomatoes! Is there no even any bread?	
ALEC:	Nothin.	
DAVIE:	Can ah take a couple ae yer crisps?	
50 ALEC:	Help yerself.	
DAVIE:	Just a couple. (*Eats crisps, swigs Irn Bru from bottle*) Reamin swats!	
	There was this lassie there. In the company like. Peggy her name was. Friend ae Kenny's.	
	Helluva nice tae talk tae. Know what ah mean? Just a really nice person.	
ALEC:	Oh aye. (*Bangs down book*)	

MARKS

5 Identify **four** ways by which the dramatist makes it clear in lines 1–23 that Alec is annoyed with his father.

4

6 By referring to **two** examples in lines 26–38, explain how the way Davie speaks is typical of someone who is slightly drunk.

4

7 Show how the tension between Alec and his father is conveyed by the way they speak in lines 39–54

4

8 Do you think Davie is a good parent or not? By referring to the extract and to elsewhere in the play, show how the dramatist makes you feel this way.

8

Text 3 – Drama

If you choose this text you may not attempt a question on Drama in Section 2.

Read the extract below and then attempt the following questions.

Tally's Blood *by Ann Marie Di Mambro*

The extract is from Act Two, Scene Five. Rosinella confronts Lucia over Hughie's letter.

ROSINELLA: What's this, eh? He's writing to you now, eh?

Rosinella opens it, takes it out.

ROSINELLA: I knew it. It's a letter.

She looks at it: frustrated because she can't read: thrusts it back at Lucia.

5 ROSINELLA: What's it say?

 LUCIA: I don't know – it doesn't matter. I'll just chuck it.

 ROSINELLA: I want to know what it says. Read it for me.

 LUCIA: Auntie Rosinella, I don't know what's wrong with you these days.

 ROSINELLA: Just read it.

10 *Lucia starts to read letter: she has to think on her feet.*

 LUCIA: It's just … just a letter.

 ROSINELLA: What's it say?

 LUCIA: It just says … it just says … Have I heard the new Guy Mitchell …? It's really good … he says … and eh … Would I ask my Uncle Massimo to get it for the juke box …? Because he thinks it
15   would be good … for the customers … So he does … and so do I … as well … I think so too.

 ROSINELLA: I don't believe you.

 LUCIA: No, it is good. You not heard it? (*Sings/tries to cajole*) 'I never felt more like singing the blues, 'cause I never thought that I'd ever lose your love, dear. You got me singing the blues. I never felt more like …'

20 ROSINELLA: Give me that. (*Grabs letter*)

 LUCIA: (*Pleading*) Auntie Rosinella.

 ROSINELLA: Don't you 'Auntie Rosinella' me. I didn't want to have to do this but you're making me. I want you to stay away from that Hughie Devlin, you hear?

 LUCIA: But why?

25 ROSINELLA: I don't want you seeing him.

 LUCIA: Hughie's my pal.

 ROSINELLA: I don't want you talking to him.

 LUCIA: I don't understand.

 ROSINELLA: Just stay away.

30 LUCIA: I won't. You can't make me.

 ROSINELLA: Alright then, lady, I'll fix you. I'll get rid of him.

 LUCIA: (*Shocked*) You wouldn't.

 ROSINELLA: I would in a minute. Jumped up wee piece of nothing thinks because he works here he can look at you. Him?

35 LUCIA: You'd do that to Hughie?

 ROSINELLA: And you'd thank me for it one day. You think I brought you up to throw yourself away on the likes of him?

 LUCIA: I can't believe you're saying this. (*A beat*) You've changed, Auntie Rosinella.

Text 2 – Prose

If you choose this text you may not attempt a question on Prose in Section 2.

Read the extract below and then attempt the following questions.

The Testament of Gideon Mack *by James Robertson*

The extract is from Chapter 33. Elsie has just left the Manse after refusing to believe what Gideon tells her about the Stone.

A crisis was upon me. I was sweating, seething with energy. If I didn't do something the energy would burst out of me and leave me wrecked on the floor. My left arm was twitching as if in contact with an electric fence. I wanted to go to the Stone, yet at the same time was afraid to go. It seemed to me that the Stone had provoked this crisis, had engineered it in some way. I paced round the manse, in and out of every room, up and down
5   the stairs. I'd just decided to get changed and head off for a long run, to try to calm down, when the bell rang again. I thought Elsie must have come back and rushed to the front door. A car had pulled up in the drive, but not Elsie's. It was Lorna Sprott.

'Gideon,' Lorna said. 'I've been at the museum. I missed the exhibition opening but I've had a good look round.' Something in my expression stopped her. 'Is this an awkward moment?'

10   'Actually, I was about to go for a run.'

'You wouldn't like to come for a walk instead? I've got Jasper in the car. I was thinking we might go to the Black Jaws.'

I opened my mouth to make an excuse, but she didn't notice.

'The exhibition surprised me,' she said. 'I didn't think it would be my cup of tea at all, and I can't say I
15   understood everything, but it was quite thought-provoking. I saw old Menteith's study and listened to you reading while I was looking down through that window. That's what put me in mind to go to the Black Jaws, the real place. I haven't been there for ages, and Jasper could do with a change from the beach.'

She looked pleadingly at me. How could I resist? Lorna stood on the step, inexorable and solid, and I knew I'd never get rid of her. Even if I slammed the door in her face she wouldn't leave me alone. I imagined her scraping
20   and chapping at the windows until I let her in. 'Wait a minute,' I said, and went to get my boots and a jacket.

Perhaps I was meant to go for a walk with Lorna, to talk to her about what was going on. Perhaps the Stone was wielding some strange power over events and had brought her to my door at this moment. In the minute or two it took me to get ready I made a decision. I would go with Lorna to the Black Jaws and, depending on how things went, I would swear her to secrecy, take her to Keldo Woods, and show her the Stone. I could trust her
25   thus far, I knew. If Lorna acknowledged that the Stone existed, then I would know I was neither hallucinating nor mad and I would go to Elsie and John. I would confront them with the misery and mockery of our lives and ask them to have the courage, with me, to change them. If, on the other hand, Lorna could not see the Stone, then I would have to admit that what Elsie had said was true, that I needed help.

MARKS

17   Show how two examples of the writer's language in lines 1–7 illustrate the idea that Gideon is in a 'crisis'.   **4**

18   By referring to lines 8–20, explain two impressions the reader is given of Lorna's character.   **4**

19   By referring to lines 21–28, show that Gideon's thinking is both rational and irrational.   **4**

20   By referring to the extract and to elsewhere in the novel, show how the writer explores Gideon's relationships with women. (You should refer in your answer to at least two female characters.)   **8**

Text 3 – Prose

If you choose this text you may not attempt a question on Prose in Section 2.

Read the extract below and then attempt the following questions.

Dr Jekyll and Mr Hyde *by Robert Louis Stevenson*

The extract is from Chapter 9, 'Dr Lanyon's Narrative'. Hyde has come to Lanyon's home and been given the chemicals. He asks for and is given a measuring glass.

He thanked me with a smiling nod, measured out a few minims of the red tincture and added one of the powders. The mixture, which was at first of a reddish hue, began, in proportion as the crystals melted, to brighten in colour, to effervesce audibly, and to throw off small fumes of vapour. Suddenly and at the same moment, the ebullition ceased and the compound changed to a dark purple, which faded again more slowly to
5   a watery green. My visitor, who had watched these metamorphoses with a keen eye, smiled, set down the glass upon the table, and then turned and looked upon me with an air of scrutiny.

"And now," said he, "to settle what remains. Will you be wise? will you be guided? will you suffer me to take this glass in my hand and to go forth from your house without further parley? or has the greed of curiosity too much command of you? Think before you answer, for it shall be done as you decide. As you decide, you shall be left
10   as you were before, and neither richer nor wiser, unless the sense of service rendered to a man in mortal distress may be counted as a kind of riches of the soul. Or, if you shall so prefer to choose, a new province of knowledge and new avenues to fame and power shall be laid open to you, here, in this room, upon the instant; and your sight shall be blasted by a prodigy to stagger the unbelief of Satan."

"Sir," said I, affecting a coolness that I was far from truly possessing, "you speak enigmas, and you will perhaps
15   not wonder that I hear you with no very strong impression of belief. But I have gone too far in the way of inexplicable services to pause before I see the end."

"It is well," replied my visitor. "Lanyon, you remember your vows: what follows is under the seal of our profession. And now, you who have so long been bound to the most narrow and material views, you who have denied the virtue of transcendental medicine, you who have derided your superiors – behold!"

20   He put the glass to his lips and drank at one gulp. A cry followed; he reeled, staggered, clutched at the table and held on, staring with injected eyes, gasping with open mouth; and as I looked there came, I thought, a change – he seemed to swell – his face became suddenly black and the features seemed to melt and alter – and the next moment, I had sprung to my feet and leaped back against the wall, my arm raised to shield me from that prodigy, my mind submerged in terror.

25   "O God!" I screamed, and "O God!" again and again; for there before my eyes – pale and shaken, and half-fainting, and groping before him with his hands, like a man restored from death – there stood Henry Jekyll!

MARKS

21   Using your own words as far as possible, summarise what happens in the extract. You should make **four** key points.   **4**

22   Look at lines 1–6.
Explain how **one** example of the writer's language in these lines creates a vivid picture of the process.   **2**

23   Look at lines 7–13.
Using your own words as far as possible, explain the choice that Hyde gives to Lanyon.
You should make **two** key points in your answer.   **2**

24   Look at lines 20–26.
By referring to **two** examples from these lines, explain how the writer creates a dramatic atmosphere.   **4**

25   With reference to this extract and to elsewhere in the novel, show how the writer uses dramatic moments to create a powerful mystery story.   **8**

Text 4 – Prose

If you choose this text you may not attempt a question on Prose in Section 2.

Read the extract below and then attempt the following questions.

The Telegram *by Iain Crichton Smith*

The extract is from the end of *The Telegram*.

'He has passed your house,' said the thin woman in a distant firm voice, and she looked up. He was walking along and he had indeed passed her house. She wanted to stand up and dance all round the kitchen, all fifteen stone of her, and shout and cry and sing a song but then she stopped. She couldn't do that. How could she do that when it must be the thin woman's son? There was no other house. The thin woman was looking out at the

5 elder, her lips pressed closely together, white and bloodless. Where had she learnt that self-control? She wasn't crying or shaking. She was looking out at something she had always dreaded but she wasn't going to cry or surrender or give herself away to anyone.

And at that moment the fat woman saw. She saw the years of discipline, she remembered how thin and unfed and pale the thin woman had always looked, how sometimes she had had to borrow money, even a shilling to

10 buy food. She saw what it must have been like to be a widow bringing up a son in a village not her own. She saw it so clearly that she was astounded. It was as if she had an extra vision, as if the air itself brought the past with all its details nearer. The number of times the thin woman had been ill and people had said that she was weak and useless. She looked down at the thin woman's arm. It was so shrivelled, and dry.

And the elder walked on. A few yards now till he reached the plank. But the thin woman hadn't cried. She was

15 steady and still, her lips still compressed, sitting upright in her chair. And, miracle of miracles, the elder passed the plank and walked straight on.

They looked at each other. What did it all mean? Where was the elder going, clutching his telegram in his hand, walking like a man in a daze? There were no other houses so where was he going? They drank their tea in silence, turning away from each other. The fat woman said, 'I must be going.' They parted for the moment

20 without speaking. The thin woman still sat at the window looking out. Once or twice the fat woman made as if to turn back as if she had something to say, some message to pass on, but she didn't. She walked away.

It wasn't till later that night that they discovered what had happened. The elder had a telegram directed to himself, to tell him of the drowning of his own son. He should never have seen it just like that, but there had been a mistake at the post office, owing to the fact that there were two boys in the village with the same name.

25 His walk through the village was a somnambulistic wandering. He didn't want to go home and tell his wife what had happened. He was walking along not knowing where he was going when later he was stopped half way to the next village. Perhaps he was going in search of his son. Altogether he had walked six miles. The telegram was crushed in his fingers and so sweaty that they could hardly make out the writing.

MARKS

26 Look at lines 1–7. Explain briefly in your own words why the fat woman wanted 'to stand up and dance all round the kitchen', **and** why she did not do so. — **2**

27 **a)** 'And at that moment the fat woman saw.' (line 8) referring to lines 8–13, explain in your own words what it was she 'saw'. — **2**

b) Explain how **two** examples of the writer's use of language in lines 8–13 emphasise the impact it has on the fat woman. — **4**

28 Explain **two** ways in which the language used in lines 17–21 creates a tense mood. — **4**

29 By referring to the extract and to at least one other story by Iain Crichton Smith, show how he ends his stories in a surprising or thought-provoking way. — **8**

Text 5 – Prose

If you choose this text you may not attempt a question on Prose in Section 2.

Read the extract below and then attempt the following questions.

Hieroglyphics *by Anne Donovan*

Ah mind they were birlin and dancin roond like big black spiders. A couldnae keep a haunle on them fur every time ah thoat ah'd captured them, tied them thegither in some kindy order they jist kep on escapin.

Just learn the rules pet. Just learn them off by heart.

5 But they didnae follow oany rules that ah could make sense of. M-A-R-Y. That's ma name. Merry. But that wus spelt different fae Merry Christmas that you wrote in the cards you made oot a folded up bits a cardboard an yon glittery stuff that comes in thae wee tubes. You pit the glue on the card and shake the glitter and it's supposed tae stick in a nice wee design. It wisnae ma fault, ah didnae mean tae drap the whole load ae it on the flerr. But how come flerr wisnae spelt the same as merry and sterr wis different again and ma heid wis nippin wi coff an laff and though and bow, meanin a bit aff a tree. Ah thoat it wis Miss Mackay that wis aff her tree, right 10 enough.

A pride of lions

A gaggle of geese

A flock of sheep

A plague of locusts

15 We hud tae learn aw they collective nouns aff by hert, chantin roond the class every afternoon when we came back in fae wur dinner, sittin wi oor erms foldit lookin oot the high windaes at the grey bloacks a flats and the grey streets, and sometimes the sky wisnae grey but maistly it wis. And ah could of tellt you the collective noun for every bliddy animal in the world practically, but it wis a bitty a waste when you think on it. Ah mean it would of come in handy if Drumchapel ever got overrun wi lions. You could of lookt oot the windae at some big hairy 20 orange beast devourin yer wee sister and turn to yer mammy and say,

Look mammy, oor Catherine's been et by a pride of lions

and huv the comfort a knowin ye were usin the correct terminology, but ah huv tae tell you it never happened. No even a floacky sheep ever meandered doon Kinfauns Drive of a Friday evenin (complete wi Mary and her little lamb who had mistaken their way). In fact ah never seen any animals barrin Alsatian dugs and scabby auld 25 cats till the trip tae the Calderpark Zoo in Primary Four.

MARKS

30 Look at lines 1–10.

By referring to **two** examples from these lines, explain how the narrator shows that she finds reading and writing confusing.

4

31 Look at lines 11–25.

By referring to **two** examples from these lines, explain how the narrator shows that school was an unpleasant experience for her.

4

32 By referring to any **two** examples from the extract as a whole, explain how the narrator's sense of humour comes across.

4

33 By referring to this story and to at least one other story by Anne Donovan, show how she explores characters who feel lonely and isolated.

8

Part C – Scottish Text – Poetry

Text 1 – Poetry

If you choose this text you may not attempt a question on Poetry in Section 2.

Read the poem below and then attempt the following questions.

Originally *by Carol Ann Duffy*

We came from our own country in a red room
which fell through the fields, our mother singing
our father's name to the turn of the wheels.
My brothers cried, one of them bawling *Home,*
5 *Home,* as the miles rushed back to the city,
the street, the house, the vacant rooms
where we didn't live any more. I stared
at the eyes of a blind toy, holding its paw.

All childhood is an emigration. Some are slow,
10 leaving you standing, resigned, up an avenue
where no one you know stays. Others are sudden.
Your accent wrong. Corners, which seem familiar,
leading to unimagined, pebble-dashed estates, big boys
eating worms and shouting words you don't understand.
15 My parents' anxiety stirred like a loose tooth
in my head. *I want our own country,* I said.

But then you forget, or don't recall, or change,
and, seeing your brother swallow a slug, feel only
a skelf of shame. I remember my tongue
20 shedding its skin like a snake, my voice
in the classroom sounding just like the rest. Do I only think
I lost a river, culture, speech, sense of first space
and the right place? Now, *Where do you come from?*
strangers ask. *Originally?* And I hesitate.

	MARKS
34 Summarise the key things that happen to the speaker of this poem. Make **four** points.	4
35 By referring to **two** examples from lines 9–14, show how the poet's use of language makes a clear distinction between 'slow' and 'sudden' emigration.	4
36 By referring to **two** examples from lines 17–24, show how the poet conveys the speaker's feelings of uncertainty.	4
37 By referring to this poem and to at least one other poem by Carol Ann Duffy, show how she creates a strong sense of character.	8

Text 2 – Poetry

If you choose this text you may not attempt a question on Poetry in Section 2.

Read the extract below and then attempt the following questions.

In the Snack-bar *by Edwin Morgan*

The extract is from In the Snack-bar *(the last 29 lines).*

I press the pedal of the drier, draw his hands
gently into the roar of the hot air.
But he cannot rub them together,
drags out a handkerchief to finish.
5   He is glad to leave the contraption, and face the stairs.
He climbs, and steadily enough.
He climbs, we climb. He climbs
with many pauses but with that one
persisting patience of the undefeated
10 which is the nature of man when all is said.
And slowly we go up. And slowly we go up.
The faltering, unfaltering steps
take him at last to the door
across that endless, yet not endless waste of floor.
15 I watch him helped on a bus. It shudders off in the rain.
The conductor bends to hear where he wants to go.

Wherever he could go it would be dark
and yet he must trust men.
Without embarrassment or shame
20 he must announce his most pitiful needs
in a public place. No one sees his face.
Does he know how frightening he is in his strangeness
under his mountainous coat, his hands like wet leaves
stuck to the half-white stick?
25 His life depends on many who would evade him.
But he cannot reckon up the chances,
having one thing to do,
to haul his blind hump through these rains of August.
Dear Christ, to be born for this!

MARKS

38 Summarise in your own words what happens in this part of the poem. Make at least **four** key points.

4

39 By referring to one example, show how the poet makes effective use of repetition in lines 6–11.

2

40 Look at lines 12–14. Explain what you think the poet means by **either** 'faltering, unfaltering' **or** 'endless, yet not endless'.

2

41 Show how **two** examples of the poet's use of language in lines 17–29 create sympathy for the old man.

4

42 By referring to this poem, and to at least one other poem by Edwin Morgan, show how he uses language to create a character or a place or an event.

8

Text 3 – Poetry

If you choose this text you may not attempt a question on Poetry in Section 2.

Read the poem below and then attempt the following questions.

Assisi *by Norman MacCaig*

The dwarf with his hands on backwards
sat, slumped like a half-filled sack
on tiny twisted legs from which
sawdust might run,
5 outside the three tiers of churches built
in honour of St Francis, brother
of the poor, talker with birds, over whom
he had the advantage
of not being dead yet.

10 A priest explained
how clever it was of Giotto
to make his frescoes tell stories
that would reveal to the illiterate the goodness
of God and the suffering
15 of His Son. I understood
the explanation and
the cleverness.

A rush of tourists, clucking contentedly,
fluttered after him as he scattered
20 the grain of the Word. It was they who had passed
the ruined temple outside, whose eyes
wept pus, whose back was higher
than his head, whose lopsided mouth
said *Grazie* in a voice as sweet
25 as a child's when she speaks to her mother
or a bird's when it spoke
to St Francis.

		MARKS
43	By referring to **two** examples of poetic techniques in lines 1–9, explain how the poet creates a vivid impression of the dwarf.	4
44	By referring to **two** examples of the poet's use of language in lines 18–20, explain how his contempt for the tourists is conveyed.	4
45	By referring to the poet's use of language in lines 20–27, show how he conveys contrasting impressions of the dwarf.	4
46	By referring to this poem and to at least one other poem by Norman MacCaig, show how he creates feelings of sympathy in the reader.	8

Text 4 – Poetry

If you choose this text you may not attempt a question on Poetry in Section 2.

Read the extract below and then attempt the following questions.

Keeping Orchids *by Jackie Kay*

The extract is from Keeping Orchids *(the first 17 lines).*

The orchids my mother gave me when we first met

are still alive, twelve days later. Although
some of the buds remain closed as secrets.

Twice since I carried them back, like a baby in a shawl,
5   from her train station to mine, then home. Twice

since then the whole glass carafe has crashed
falling over, unprovoked, soaking my chest of drawers.

All the broken waters. I have rearranged
the upset orchids with troubled hands. Even after

10   that the closed ones did not open out. The skin
shut like an eye in the dark; the closed lid.

Twelve days later, my mother's hands are all I have.
Her face is fading fast. Even her voice rushes

through a tunnel the other way from home.
15   I close my eyes and try to remember exactly:

a paisley pattern scarf, a brooch, a navy coat.
A digital watch her daughter was wearing when she died.

			MARKS
47	**a)**	Look at lines 1–11. Using your own words as far as possible, identify **four** ways in which the speaker's behaviour makes it clear that the orchids are important to her.	4
	b)	Show how the poet's language conveys the idea that the orchids are a little mysterious. Refer to **two** examples in your answer.	4
48		By referring to lines 12–17, show how the poet's language emphasises the difficulty the speaker has remembering her mother. Refer to **two** examples in your answer.	4
49		By referring to this poem and to at least one other poem by Jackie Kay, show how she explores the theme of isolation.	8

[End of Section 1]

Section 2 – Critical Essay – 20 marks

Attempt **ONE** question from the following genres – Drama, Prose, Poetry, Film and Television Drama, or Language.

Your answer must be on a different genre from that chosen in Section 1.

You should spend approximately 45 minutes on this Section.

Drama

Answers to questions on Drama should refer to the text and to such relevant features as characterisation, key scene(s), structure, climax, theme, plot, conflict, setting …

1   Choose a play in which there is a character who suffers from a human weakness such as jealousy, pride, ambition, selfishness, lust.

   By referring to appropriate techniques, show how the weakness is revealed, and then explain how this weakness affects both the characters and the events of the play.

2   Choose a scene from a play in which suspense or tension is built up.
   By referring to appropriate techniques, show how this suspense or tension is built up and what effect this scene has on the play as a whole.

Prose

Answers to questions on Prose should refer to the text and to such relevant features as characterisation, setting, language, key incident(s), climax, turning point, plot, structure, narrative technique, theme, ideas, description …

3   Choose a novel **or** a short story in which there is a character you admire or dislike or feel sorry for.

   By referring to appropriate techniques, show how the author creates this character, and say why you feel this way about him/her.

4   Choose a novel **or** a short story **or** a work of non-fiction that explores a theme which you think is important.

   By referring to appropriate techniques, show how the author explores this theme.

Poetry

Answers to questions on Poetry should refer to the text and to such relevant features as word choice, tone, imagery, structure, content, rhythm, rhyme, theme, sound, ideas …

5   Choose a poem which presents a memorable picture of a person or of a place.
   By referring to poetic techniques, explain how the poet makes the picture memorable.

6   Choose a poem which made you think more deeply about an aspect of life you think is important.
   By referring to poetic techniques, show how the poet explores this aspect of life.

Film and Television Drama

Answers to questions on Film and Television Drama should refer to the text and to such relevant features as use of camera, key sequence, characterisation, mise-en-scène, editing, setting, music/sound, special effects, plot, dialogue …

7   Choose a scene or sequence from a film **or** television drama* in which tension is created.

By referring to appropriate techniques, explain how the tension is created.

8   Choose a film **or** television drama* which has a character who can be described as a hero or as a villain or as a mixture of both.

By referring to appropriate techniques, explain how the character is presented in the film or television drama.*

* 'television drama' includes a single play, a series or a serial.

Language

Answers to questions on Language should refer to the text and to such relevant features as register, accent, dialect, slang, jargon, vocabulary, tone, abbreviation …

9   Choose a text which you consider to be persuasive, for example an advertisement or a speech or a newspaper column.

By referring to specific examples, explain how successful the persuasive language is.

10 Consider the specialist language used by a group of people to talk about a particular topic, for example a sport or a job or a hobby or a pastime.

By referring to specific examples and to appropriate techniques, explain how the specialist language used by the group is effective in communicating ideas clearly.

[End of Practice Paper 1]

Reading for Understanding, Analysis and Evaluation

The real price of gold

Like many of his Inca ancestors, Juan Apaza is possessed by gold. Descending into an icy tunnel 17,000 feet up in the Peruvian Andes, the 44-year-old miner stuffs a wad of coca leaves into his mouth to brace himself for the inevitable hunger and fatigue. For 30 days each month Apaza toils, without pay, deep inside this mine dug down under a glacier above the world's highest town, La Rinconada. For 30 days he faces the dangers that have

5   killed many of his fellow miners – explosives, toxic gases, tunnel collapses – to extract the gold that the world demands. Apaza does all this, without pay, so that he can make it to today, the 31st day, when he and his fellow miners are given a single shift, four hours or maybe a little more, to haul out and keep as much rock as their weary shoulders can bear. Under the ancient system that still prevails in the high Andes, this is what passes for a pay cheque: a sack of rocks that may contain a small fortune in gold or, far more often, very little at all.

10   For more than 500 years the glittering seams trapped beneath the glacial ice here, three miles above sea level, have drawn people to this place in Peru. First the Inca, then the Spanish, whose lust for gold and silver spurred the conquest of the New World. But it is only now, as the price of gold soars – it has risen 235 percent in the past eight years – that 30,000 people have flocked to La Rinconada, turning a lonely prospectors' camp into a squalid shantytown on top of the world. Fuelled by luck and desperation, sinking in its own toxic waste and

15   lawlessness, this no-man's-land now teems with dreamers and schemers anxious to strike it rich, even if it means destroying their environment – and themselves – in the process.

Only gold, that object of desire and destruction, could have conjured up a place of such startling contradictions as La Rinconada. Remote and inhospitable – at 17,000 feet, even oxygen is in short supply – the town is, nevertheless, growing at a furious pace. Approaching the settlement from across the high plains, a visitor first

20   sees the glint of rooftops under a magnificent glacier draped like a wedding veil across the mountain. Then comes the stench. It's not just the garbage dumped down the slope, but the human and industrial waste that clogs the settlement's streets.

The scene may sound almost medieval, but La Rinconada is one of the frontiers of a thoroughly modern phenomenon: a 21st-century gold rush.

25   No single element has tantalized and tormented the human imagination more than the shimmering metal known by the chemical symbol Au. For thousands of years the desire to possess gold has driven people to extremes, fuelling wars and conquests, underpinning empires and currencies, levelling mountains and forests. Gold is not vital to human existence; it has, in fact, relatively few practical uses. Yet its chief virtues – its unusual density and its imperishable shine – have made it one of the world's most coveted commodities, a transcendent

30   symbol of beauty, wealth, and immortality. From pharaohs (who insisted on being buried in what they called the 'flesh of the gods') to the forty-niners (whose mad rush for the mother lode built the American West) to the financiers (who made it the bedrock of the global economy): nearly every society through the ages has invested gold with an almost mythological power.

For all of its allure, gold's human and environmental toll has never been so steep. Part of the challenge, as

35   well as the fascination, is that there is so little of it. In all of history, only 161,000 tons of gold have been mined, barely enough to fill two Olympic-size swimming pools. More than half of that has been extracted in the past

50 years. Now the world's richest deposits are fast being depleted, and new discoveries are rare. Gone are the hundred-mile-long gold reefs in South Africa or cherry-size nuggets in California. Most of the gold left to mine exists as traces buried in remote and fragile corners of the globe. It's an invitation to destruction. But there is no
40 shortage of miners, big and small, who are willing to accept.

At one end of the spectrum are the armies of poor migrant workers converging on small-scale mines like La Rinconada. Employing crude methods that have hardly changed in centuries, they produce about 25 percent of the world's gold. At the other end of the spectrum are vast, open-pit mines run by the world's largest mining companies. Using armadas of supersize machines, these big-footprint mines produce three-quarters of the
45 world's gold.

Gold mining, however, generates more waste per ounce than any other metal, and the mines' mind-bending disparities of scale show why: these gashes in the Earth are so massive they can be seen from space, yet the particles being mined in them are so microscopic that, in many cases, more than 200 could fit on the head of a pin. There is no avoiding the brutal calculus of gold mining: extracting a single ounce of gold – the amount in a
50 typical wedding ring – requires the removal of more than 250 tons of rock and ore.

Back in La Rinconada, Apaza is still waiting for a stroke of luck. 'Maybe today will be the big one,' he says. To improve his odds, the miner has already made his 'payment to the Earth': a bottle of pisco, the local liquor, placed near the mouth of the mine; a few coca leaves slipped under a rock; and, several months back, a rooster sacrificed on the sacred mountaintop. Now, heading into the tunnel, he mumbles a prayer in his native Quechua
55 language to the deity who rules the mountain and all the gold within.

Brook Larmer, in *National Geographic* magazine (adapted)

		MARKS
1	Look at lines 1–9. Explain **in your own words four** things that make Juan Apaza's working life harsh.	4
2	Look at lines 10–16. Explain how **two** examples of the writer's **word choice** demonstrate how unpleasant La Rinconada has become.	4
3	Look at lines 17–22. Explain how the language used demonstrates that La Rinconada is 'a place of … contradictions'. You should give **two** examples in your answer.	4
4	Explain why the sentence 'The scene … gold rush' (lines 23–24) provides an appropriate link at this point in the passage.	2
5	Look at lines 25–33. Summarise, **using your own words** as far as possible, some of the points made about gold. You should make **five** key points in your answer.	5
6	Look at lines 34–40. Explain **in your own words** why it is difficult to mine gold today. You should give **three** examples in your answer.	3
7	Look at lines 41–55. Explain how **two** examples of the language used demonstrate the destructive nature of gold mining.	4
8	Look at lines 46–50. Explain **in your own words** what the writer means by 'disparities of scale'.	2
9	Explain why the last paragraph (lines 51–55) provides an effective conclusion to the passage as a whole.	2

[End of question paper]

Critical Reading

Duration: 90 minutes

Total marks: 40

SECTION 1 – Scottish Text – 20 marks

Read an extract from a Scottish text you have previously studied.

Choose ONE text from either

Drama

or

Prose

or

Poetry

Attempt ALL the questions for your chosen text.

SECTION 2 – Critical Essay – 20 marks

Attempt ONE question from the following genres – Drama, Prose, Poetry, Film and Television Drama, or Language.

Your answer must be on a different genre from that chosen in Section 1.

You should spend approximately 45 minutes on each Section.

Write your answers clearly in the answer booklet provided. In the answer booklet you must clearly identify the question number you are attempting.

Use **blue** or **black** ink.

Before leaving the examination room you must give your answer booklet to the Invigilator; if you do not, you may lose all the marks for this paper.

Section 1 – Scottish Text – 20 marks

Part A – Scottish Text – Drama

Text 1 – Drama

If you choose this text you may not attempt a question on Drama in Section 2.

Read the extract below and then attempt the following questions.

Bold Girls *by Rona Munro*

The extract is from Scene One. Deirdre appears in Marie's house for the first time.

Deirdre comes into the room. She stands uncertain in the centre of the room.

Marie enters behind her.

The three older women just stare at Deirdre.

DEIRDRE: Can I stay here till I'm dry, Mrs? They won't let me up the road.

There is a pause then Marie finally stirs

MARIE: You better sit down by the fire (*She switches on the TV*)

Deirdre sits by the fire

5 *Nora, Marie and Cassie slowly sit as well, watching her*

NORA: I don't know your face.

Deirdre says nothing. She doesn't look up from the fire

     Well where are you from?

Deirdre jerks her head without turning

10 Where?

DEIRDRE: (*sullen, quietly*) Back of the school there.

NORA: What's that?

DEIRDRE: (*loudly*) Back of the school there.

NORA: Those houses next the off-licence?

15 *Deirdre nods*

I know where you are. So what happened to you then?

Deirdre shrugs. She looks up and catches Cassie's eye

Cassie turns quickly to look at the TV

MARIE: Will you take a cup of tea, love?

20 *Deirdre nods*

Marie goes to make it

Nora stares at Deirdre a while longer, then turns to Cassie

NORA: So Cassie, looks like that wee brother of yours will miss his tea altogether?

CASSIE: (*with her eyes on the TV*) Looks like he might.

25 NORA: I hope he's the sense to stay in town.

CASSIE: Sure he'll phone next door, let us know what's happening.

NORA: Aye he's a good boy.

There is a pause while everyone watches the TV in an uncomfortable silence

Marie brings Deirdre the tea and some biscuits. Deirdre takes it without saying anything, starts to eat and drink
30 *furtively and ravenously. Cassie and Marie exchange glances over her head*

MARIE: Turn the sound up on that will you, Nora?

		MARKS
1	By referring to the whole extract, identify **four** ways in which Deirdre's behaviour makes her appear strange.	4
2	Describe the way each of the **three** older women treats Deirdre. Support your answers with three references to the text.	6
3	Why do you think Marie asks Nora to turn up the sound on the TV? (line 31)	2
4	By referring to this extract and to the play as a whole, show how the role of Deirdre is important in the play.	8

Text 2 – Drama

If you choose this text you may not attempt a question on Drama in Section 2.

Read the extract below and then attempt the following questions.

Sailmaker *by Alan Spence*

The extract is from Act One. Davie and Billy discuss money problems.

(*Enter* DAVIE *and* BILLY, *talking as they walk*)

DAVIE:	Eh, Billy … that coupla quid ah tapped off ye. Could it wait till next week?
BILLY:	Aye sure.
DAVIE:	Things are still a wee bit tight.
BILLY:	What's the score?
DAVIE:	Eh?
BILLY:	Ye shouldnae be this skint. What is it?
DAVIE:	Ah told ye. It's the job. Just hasnae been so great. No sellin enough. No collectin enough. No gettin much over the basic.
BILLY:	Aye, but ye should be able tae get by. Just the two ae ye.
DAVIE:	It's no easy.
BILLY:	Ye bevvyin?
DAVIE:	Just a wee half when ah finish ma work. An by Christ ah need it.
BILLY:	Ye bettin too heavy? Is that it?
DAVIE:	(*Hesitates then decides to tell him*) It started a coupla months ago. Backed a favourite. Absolute surefire certainty. Couldnae lose. But it was even money, so ah had tae put quite a whack on it. (*Slightly shamefaced*) Best part ae a week's wages.
BILLY:	An it got beat?
DAVIE:	Out the park. So ah made it up by borrowin off the bookie. He does his moneylender on the side. Charges interest.
BILLY:	An every week ye miss the interest goes up.
DAVIE:	This is it. Now when ah pay him ah'm just clearin the interest. Ah'm no even touchin the original amount ah borrowed. Ah must've paid him back two or three times over, an ah still owe him the full whack.
BILLY:	Bastard, eh? Sicken ye. And he's a pape.
	(DAVIE *laughs*)
DAVIE:	Still, Aw ah need's a wee turn. Ah mean ma luck's got tae change sometime hasn't it? Law of averages.
BILLY:	Whatever that is.
DAVIE:	Things have got tae get better.
BILLY:	It's a mug's game. The punter canny win.
DAVIE:	Got tae keep tryin.
BILLY:	Flingin it away!
	Look, Don't get me wrong. Ah don't mind helpin ye out, but ah'm no exactly rollin in it maself.
DAVIE:	You'll get yer money back.
BILLY:	That's no what ah mean!
DAVIE:	What am ah supposed tae dae? Get a job as a company director or somethin! Ah'll go doon tae the broo in the mornin!
BILLY:	There must be some way tae get this bookie aff yer back for a start.
DAVIE:	Aye sure!
BILLY:	Ah mean, you've *paid* him.
DAVIE:	Ah knew his terms.
BILLY:	It's no even legal.

Part B – Scottish Text – Prose

Text 1 – Prose

If you choose this text you may not attempt a question on Prose in Section 2.

Read the extract below and then attempt the following questions.

The Cone-Gatherers *by Robin Jenkins*

The extract is from Chapter 11. Calum and Neil are in a tree when a storm begins and they climb down to seek shelter.

The brothers crept slowly downward. Every time lightning flashed and thunder crashed they thought their tree had been shattered, and clung, helpless as woodlice, waiting to be hurled to the ground with the fragments. The tree itself seemed to be terrified; every branch, every twig, heaved and slithered. At times it seemed to have torn its roots in its terror and to be dangling in the air.

5   At last they reached the ground. At once Neil flung his bag of cones down and snatched up his knapsack. He shouted to Calum to do likewise.

'We'd never get to the hut alive,' he gasped. 'We'd get killed among the trees. Forby, it's too far away. We're going to the beach hut.'

'But we're not allowed, Neil.'

10   Neil clutched his brother and spoke to him as calmly as he could.

'I ken it's not allowed, Calum,' he said. 'I ken we gave our promise to Mr. Tulloch not to get into any more trouble. But look at the rain. We're soaked already. I've got rheumatics, and you ken your chest is weak. If we shelter under a tree it might get struck by lightning and we'd be killed. In three minutes we can reach the beach hut.'

15   'But we promised, Neil. The lady will be angry again.'

'Do you want me then to be a useless cripple for the rest of my days? What if she is angry? All she can do is to tell us to leave her wood, and I'll be glad to go. I don't want you to do what you think is wrong, Calum; but sometimes we've got to choose between two things, neither of them to our liking. We'll do no harm. We'll leave the place as we find it. Nobody will ever ken we've been in it. What do you say then?'

20   Calum nodded unhappily.

'I think maybe we should go,' he said.

'All right then. We'd better run for it. But didn't I tell you to drop your cone bag?'

'They'll get all wet, Neil.'

Neil stood gaping; he saw the rain streaming down the green grime on his brother's face; beyond Calum was
25   the wood shrouded in wet.

'They'll get wet,' he heard himself repeating.

'Aye, that's right, Neil. Mind what Mr. Tulloch said, if they get wet they're spoiled.'

It was no use being bitter or angry or sarcastic.

'Is there never to be any sun again then,' cried Neil, 'to dry them?'

30   Calum looked up at the sky.

'I think so, Neil,' he murmured.

MARKS

13 Explain **two** ways in which the writer's use of language in lines 1–4 conveys the violence of the storm.

4

14 Look at lines 5–10. Show how **one** example of the writer's word choice makes clear how impatient Neil is.

2

15 Using your own words as far as possible, summarise the key points in Neil's argument to persuade Calum to go to the beach hut (lines 11–19). Make at least **four** key points.

4

16 Explain how the writer makes Calum seem childlike in lines 23–31.

2

17 By referring to this extract and to elsewhere in the novel, show how the relationship between Calum and Neil is developed.

8

Text 4 – Prose

If you choose this text you may not attempt a question on Prose in Section 2.

Read the extract below and then attempt the following questions.

Mother and Son *by Iain Crichton Smith*

The extract is from near the beginning of Mother and Son.

In the bed was a woman. She was sleeping, her mouth tightly shut and prim and anaemic. There was a bitter smile on her lips as if fixed there; just as you sometimes see the insurance man coming to the door with the same smile each day, the same brilliant smile which never falls away till he's gone into the anonymity of the streets. The forehead was not very high and not low, though its wrinkles gave it an expression of concentration
5   as if the woman were wrestling with some terrible witch's idea in dreams.

The man looked at her for a moment, then fumbled for his matches again and began to light a fire. The sticks fell out of place and he cursed vindictively and helplessly. For a moment he sat squatting on his haunches staring into the fire, as if he were thinking of some state of innocence, some state to which he could not return: a reminiscent smile dimpled his cheeks and showed in eyes which immediately became still and dangerous again.

10 The clock struck five wheezingly and, at the first chime, the woman woke up. She started as she saw the figure crouched over the fire and then subsided: 'It's only you.' There was relief in the voice, but there was a curious hint of contempt or acceptance. He still sat staring into the fire and answered dully: 'Yes, it's only me!' He couldn't be said to speak the words: they fell away from him as sometimes happens when one is in a deep reverie where every question is met by its answer almost instinctively.

15 'Well, what's the matter with you!' she snapped pettishly, 'sitting there moping with the tea to be made. I sometimes don't know why we christened you John' – with a sigh. 'My father was never like you. He was a man who knew his business.'

'All right, all right,' he said despairingly. 'Can't you get a new record for your gramophone. I've heard all that before,' as if he were conscious of the inadequacy of this familiar retort – he added: 'hundreds of times.' But she
20 wasn't to be stopped.

'I can't understand what has come over you lately. You keep mooning about the house, pacing up and down with your hands in your pockets. Do you know what's going to happen to you, you'll be taken to the asylum. That's where you'll go. Your father's people had something wrong with their heads, it was in your family but not in ours.'

MARKS

27 Explain **two** ways the language used in lines 1–5 creates an unpleasant impression of the mother.   4

28 By referring to the language used in lines 6–14, explain **two** impressions you are given of the son's character.   4

29 Show how the language used in lines 15–24 conveys the hostile atmosphere between mother and son. Refer to **two** examples in your answer.   4

30 By referring to the extract and to at least one other story by Crichton Smith, show how he explores conflict between characters.   8

Text 5 – Prose

If you choose this text you may not attempt a question on Prose in Section 2.

Read the extract below and then attempt the following questions.

Away in a Manger *by Anne Donovan*

They turned the corner and the cauld evaporated. The square shimmerin wi light, brightness sharp against the gloomy street. Trees frosted wi light. Lights shaped intae circles and flowers, like the plastic jewellery sets wee lassies love. Lights switchin on and off in a mad rhythm ae their ain, tryin tae look like bells ringin and snow fallin. Reindeer and Santas, holly, ivy, robins, all bleezin wi light. Amy gazed at them, eyes shinin.

5   'Haud ma haund tight tae we get across this road. There's lots of motors here.' Sandra pulled Amy close in tae her. 'They're lovely, aren't they?'

'Uh huh.' Amy nodded. 'Can we walk right round the square?'

A tape of Christmas carols was playin on the sound system, fillin the air like a cracklin heavenly choir. Sandra and Amy joined the other faimlies wanderin round.

10   'Look at they reindeer, Mark!'

'There's a star, Daddy!'

'Check the size a that tree!'

Amy stopped in front of the big Christmas tree in the centre of the square.

'Can we sit doon tae look at it, Mammy?'

15   'Naw, just keep walkin, pet. It's too cauld.'

Anyway, nearly every bench was occupied. Newspapers neatly smoothed oot like bedclothes. Some folk were huddled under auld coats, tryin tae sleep their way intae oblivion while others sat upright, hauf-empty cans in their haunds, starin at the passers-by. Sandra minded when she was wee and her mammy'd brought her tae see the lights. There were folk on the benches then, down-and-outs, faces shrunk wi drink and neglect, an auld cap
20   lyin hauf-heartedly by their sides. But now the people who slept in the square werenae just auld drunks and it was hard tae pick them oot fae everyone else. That couple ower there wi their bags roond them, were they just havin a rest fae their Christmas shoppin, watchin the lights? But who in their right minds would be sittin on a bench in George Square on this freezin cauld night if they'd a hame tae go tae?

Amy tugged at her airm. 'Ah know that song.'

25   'Whit song?'

'That one.' Amy pointed upwards. 'Silent Night, Holy Night.'

'Do you?'

'We learned it at school. Mrs Anderson was tellin us aboot the baby Jesus and how there was nae room at the inn so he was born in a stable.'

30   'Oh.'

'It's no ma favourite, but.'

'What's no your favourite?'

'Silent Night. Guess what ma favourite is?'

'Don't know.'

35   'Guess, Mammy, you have tae guess.'

Sandra couldnae be bothered guessin but she knew there'd be nae peace tae she'd made some attempt and anyway, Amy'd get bored wi the 'Guess what?' game quick enough.

'Little donkey?'

'Naw.'

40   'O Little Town of Bethlehem?'

      'Naw. Gie in?'

      'OK.'

      'Away in a Manger. Ah've won!' Amy jumped up and doon. 'Mammy, what's a manger?'

MARKS

31   Look at lines 1–18. By referring to **two** examples, explain how the writer's language creates a mood of excitement. — 4

32   **a)**   Look at lines 16–23. Show how **one** example of the writer's language conveys a vivid impression of the people on the benches **now**. — 2

         b)   Look at lines 16–23. Show how one example of the writer's language conveys a vivid impression of the people on the benches in **the past**. — 2

33   Look at the conversation between Sandra and her daughter in lines 24–43. By referring to **two** examples, identify **four** ways in which the conversation is typical of one between an excited child and a parent. — 4

34   By referring to the extract and to at least one other story by Anne Donovan, show how the theme of parent/child relationships is developed. — 8

Part C – Scottish Text – Poetry

Text 1 – Poetry

If you choose this text you may not attempt a question on Poetry in Section 2.

Read the poem below and then attempt the following questions.

The Way My Mother Speaks *by Carol Ann Duffy*

I say her phrases to myself

in my head

or under the shallows of my breath,

restful shapes moving.

5   *The day and ever. The day and ever.*

The train this slow evening

goes down England

browsing for the right sky,

too blue swapped for a cool grey.

10 For miles I have been saying

What like is it

the way I say things when I think.

Nothing is silent. Nothing is not silent.

What like is it.

15 Only tonight

I am happy and sad

like a child

who stood at the end of summer

and dipped a net

20 in a green, erotic pond. *The day*

and ever. The day and ever.

I am homesick, free, in love

with the way my mother speaks.

		MARKS
35	Look at lines 1–5. By referring to **two** examples from these lines, explain how the poet creates a calm mood at the start of the poem.	4
36	Look at lines 6–14. By referring to the language of these lines, explain **one** emotion the speaker is experiencing during the train journey.	2
37	Look at lines 15–20. By referring closely to these lines, explain how the simile 'like a child … pond' conveys the idea that the speaker is both 'happy' and 'sad'.	4
38	Look at lines 22–23. Explain how any part of these lines makes an effective conclusion to the poem.	2
39	By referring to this poem and to at least one other poem by Carol Ann Duffy, show how memory and recollection are important in her poems.	8

Text 2 – Poetry

If you choose this text you may not attempt a question on Poetry in Section 2.

Read the extract below and then attempt the following questions.

Glasgow 5 March 1971 *by Edwin Morgan*

With a ragged diamond
of shattered plate-glass
a young man and his girl
are falling backwards into a shop-window
5   The young man's face
is bristling with fragments of glass
and the girl's leg has caught
on the broken window
and spurts arterial blood
10   over her wet-look white coat.
Their arms are starfished out
braced for impact,
their faces show surprise, shock,
and the beginning of pain.
15   The two youths who have pushed them
are about to complete the operation
reaching into the window
to loot what they can smartly.
Their faces show no expression.
20   It is a sharp clear night
in Sauchiehall Street.
In the background two drivers
keep their eyes on the road.

		MARKS
40	Using your own words as far as possible, summarise what happens in the poem. You should make **three** key points.	3
41	Look at lines 1–14. By referring to **two** examples of the poet's use of language in these lines, explain how the poet creates a vivid picture of the event.	4
42	Look at lines 15–19. By referring to **one** example of the poet's word choice in these lines, explain what impression the poet creates of the two youths.	2
43	Look at lines 20–23. How effective do you find these lines as a conclusion to the poem? You should refer to at least one example from these lines and to the ideas of the rest of the poem.	3
44	By referring to this poem and to at least one other poem by Edwin Morgan, show how the poet evokes sympathy for people in his poems.	8

Text 3 – Poetry

If you choose this text you may not attempt a question on Poetry in Section 2.

Read the poem below and then attempt the following questions.

Basking Shark *by Norman MacCaig*

To stub an oar on a rock where none should be,
To have it rise with a slounge out of the sea
Is a thing that happened once (too often) to me.

But not too often – though enough. I count as gain
5 That I once met, on a sea tin-tacked with rain,
That roomsized monster with a matchbox brain.

He displaced more than water. He shoggled me
Centuries back – this decadent townee
Shook on a wrong branch of his family tree.

10 Swish up the dirt and, when it settles, a spring
Is all the clearer. I saw me, in one fling,
Emerging from the slime of everything.

So who's the monster? The thought made me grow pale
For twenty seconds while, sail after sail,
15 The tall fin slid away and then the tail.

		MARKS
45	By referring to the whole poem, explain in your own words what the poet's encounter with the shark made him reflect on.	2
46	By referring to lines 1–3, explain one way the poet suggests the encounter was quite alarming.	2
47	Show how any **one** poetic technique in line 6 adds impact to the description of the shark.	2
48	Choose any **two** examples of the poet's use of language in lines 7–9 which you find effective. Justify your choices in detail.	4
49	What impression does the last stanza (lines 13–15) create of the poet's feelings about the shark? Support your opinion with reference to the text.	2
50	By referring to this poem and to at least one other poem by Norman MacCaig, show how he uses imagery and striking word choice in his poems.	8

Text 4 – Poetry

If you choose this text you may not attempt a question on Poetry in Section 2.

Read the poem below and then attempt the following questions.

Lucozade *by Jackie Kay*

My mum is on a high bed next to sad chrysanthemums.
'Don't bring flowers, they only wilt and die.'
I am scared my mum is going to die
on the bed next to the sad chrysanthemums.

5 She nods off and her eyes go back in her head.
Next to her bed is a bottle of Lucozade.
'Orange nostalgia, that's what that is,' she says.
'Don't bring Lucozade either,' then fades.

'The whole day was a blur, a swarm of eyes.
10 Those doctors with their white lies.
Did you think you could cheer me up with a *Woman's Own*?
Don't bring magazines, too much about size.'

My mum wakes up, groggy and low.
'What I want to know,' she says, 'is this:
15 where's the big brandy, the generous gin, the Bloody Mary,
the biscuit tin, the chocolate gingers, the dirty big meringue?'

I am sixteen; I've never tasted a Bloody Mary.
'Tell your father to bring a luxury,' says she.
'Grapes have no imagination, they're just green.
20 Tell him: stop the neighbours coming.'

I clear her cupboard in Ward 10B, Stobhill Hospital.
I leave, bags full, Lucozade, grapes, oranges,
sad chrysanthemums under my arms,
weighted down. I turn round, wave with her flowers.

25 My mother, on her high hospital bed, waves back.
Her face is light and radiant, dandelion hours.
Her sheets billow and whirl. She is beautiful.
Next to her the empty table is divine.

I carry the orange nostalgia home singing an old song.

MARKS

51   Look at lines 1–12. Explain **two** ways the poet makes clear the mother's negative mood.

4

52   By referring to **two** examples, show how the poet's use of language in lines 13–20 makes a clear contrast between 'grapes' and the 'luxury' the mother asks for.

4

53   By referring to **two** examples of the language used in lines 21–29, show how the poem ends on a positive note.

4

54   By referring to this poem and to at least one other poem by Jackie Kay, show how she explores the theme of relationships across generations.

8

[End of Section 1]

Section 2 – Critical Essay – 20 marks

Attempt **ONE** question from the following genres – Drama, Prose, Poetry, Film and Television Drama, or Language.

Your answer must be on a different genre from that chosen in Section 1.

You should spend approximately 45 minutes on this Section.

Drama

Answers to questions on Drama should refer to the text and to such relevant features as characterisation, key scene(s), structure, climax, theme, plot, conflict, setting …

1   Choose a play in which there is conflict between characters or between groups of characters or within one character.

By referring to appropriate techniques, go on to explain why the conflict is important to the development of the play as a whole.

2   Choose a play in which there is one scene you consider to be a turning point.
By referring to appropriate techniques, go on to explain how it makes an impact on the play as a whole.

Prose

Answers to questions on Prose should refer to the text and to such relevant features as characterisation, setting, language, key incident(s), climax, turning point, plot, structure, narrative technique, theme, ideas, description …

3   Choose a novel **or** a short story which ends in a way you think is effective.
By referring to appropriate techniques, explain why you think the ending is effective.

4   Choose a novel **or** a short story **or** a work of non-fiction which deals with an important human issue (such as prejudice, the conflict between good and evil, loss of freedom, hatred between individuals or groups, abuse of power).
By referring to appropriate techniques, show how the writer explores this issue.

Poetry

Answers to questions on Poetry should refer to the text and to such relevant features as word choice, tone, imagery, structure, content, rhythm, rhyme, theme, sound, ideas …

5   Choose a poem in which the poet creates a particular mood or atmosphere.
By referring to poetic techniques, show how the poet creates this mood or atmosphere.

6   Choose a poem which describes an incident or an event or an encounter.
By referring to poetic techniques, show how the poet creates the description.

Film and Television Drama

Answers to questions on Film and Television Drama should refer to the text and to such relevant features as use of camera, key sequence, characterisation, mise-en-scène, editing, setting, music/sound, special effects, plot, dialogue …

7   Choose the opening **or** closing scene **or** sequence from a film or television drama.*

By referring to appropriate techniques, explain why you find it an effective way to start or to finish the film or television drama.*

8   Choose a film **or** television drama* in which a character has to overcome a number of difficulties.

By referring to appropriate techniques, explain how successful the character is in overcoming these difficulties.

* 'television drama' includes a single play, a series or a serial.

Language

Answers to questions on Language should refer to the text and to such relevant features as register, accent, dialect, slang, jargon, vocabulary, tone, abbreviation …

9   Consider the specialised language of any specific group of people.

By referring to specific examples and to appropriate techniques, explain in what ways the language is distinctive and what benefit(s) the group gains from the use of this language.

10   Choose a print or non-print text which sets out to persuade people.

By referring to specific examples and to appropriate techniques, explain how the text engages the reader or viewer.

[End of Practice Paper 2]

ANSWERS TO PRACTICE PAPERS

Practice Paper 1

Reading for Understanding, Analysis and Evaluation

Sport will continue to transcend the ages

Question	Expected response	Max. mark	Additional guidance
1	You should explain fully why the first paragraph is an effective opening to the passage as a whole. Be aware of and use a mixed approach (i.e. ideas and language) to this question. Any two points for 2 marks.	2	▸ it introduces the main topic of sport … (1) ▸ … and how much of it there is (1) ▸ it creates surprise/amusement at the sheer amount (1) Also accept: ▸ use of first person (1) ▸ use of list to demonstrate abundance of sport (1) ▸ understatement of 'a fair bit' (1) ▸ the density of proper names, numbers, abbreviations is almost confusing/disturbing (1)
2	You should explain in your own words four ways in which the importance of sport has changed over the years. Any four points for 4 marks.	4	▸ 30 years ago, no football on TV led to very little complaint (1) ▸ today, it would cause uproar (1) ▸ in mid-19th century, there were no major international/worldwide sporting events (1) ▸ in mid-19th century, there were no organisations set up to control sport (1) ▸ for a long time sport was not considered important (1) ▸ for a long time sport was seen by churches as an unsuitable way to spend time (1)
3	You should explain what the careers adviser's attitude was to sports journalism, and how one example of the writer's word choice makes this attitude clear. Identification of attitude (1) Reference (1) plus appropriate comment (1)	3	Identification of attitude, e.g. dismissive, contemptuous, disrespectful, scornful (1) Possible answers include: ▸ 'spluttered' (1) suggests she was taken aback, lost for words (1) ▸ 'doubted' (1) suggests she didn't think it was a viable career (1) ▸ list ('technology, video games, …') (1) suggests she thought there were many competing attractions (1) ▸ 'host of other things' (1) suggests she thought there were many alternatives to an interest in sport (1)
4	You should explain how two examples of the writer's word choice demonstrate how fierce the competition is among TV channels. Reference (1) plus appropriate comment (1) × 2	4	▸ 'drives' (1) suggests power, forcefulness (1) ▸ 'jostle' (1) suggests fighting, squabbling, jockeying for position (1) ▸ 'fever pitch' (1) suggests heightened, almost irrational activity (1) ▸ 'war' (1) suggests outright conflict, fighting (1) ▸ 'giants' (1) suggests the sheer size of the competing forces (1) ▸ 'cut the legs' (1) suggests violence, desire to maim, damage (1) ▸ 'Trojan horse' (1) suggests taking over by subterfuge, cunning/underhand way of winning (1)

Question	Expected response	Max. mark	Additional guidance
5	You should explain using your own words as far as possible five pieces of evidence the writer gives to show that the careers adviser was wrong about people's interest in sport. Any five of the points in the 'Additional guidance' column for 5 marks.	5	Glosses of: ▶ 'proliferation in radio stations', e.g. rise in number of radio stations (1) ▶ 'hundreds of podcasts and blogs', e.g. extensive personal comment on the internet (1) ▶ 'sport has colonised them [new technologies]', e.g. sport has taken them over (1) ▶ 'most prevalent theme on Twitter', e.g. the most common topic, most talked about subject (1) ▶ 'what people want to watch on a growing list of devices', e.g. what people use all the new communication technology for (1) ▶ 'vehicle to break the ice', e.g. a topic which can start off conversations, get to know someone, help people relax in social situations (1) ▶ 'allows large sections of society to come together in a shared experience', e.g. it unites groups of people with common national or cultural backgrounds (1)
6	You should explain in your own words the importance of the 'Victorian era' in changing attitudes to sport. Any two of the points in the 'Additional guidance' column for 2 marks.	2	Glosses of: ▶ it sought to 'redefine sport's moral status', e.g. change the way people saw sport as being good or bad (1) ▶ 'help young people to respect rules', e.g. encourage them to obey the regulations or procedures (1) ▶ '[help young people to] develop character', e.g. improve their personality, help them grow as (moral) individuals (1) ▶ 'spread throughout the empire', e.g. became a worldwide influence (1)
7	You should explain how two examples of the language used (such as word choice, sentence structure or imagery) demonstrate the writer's feelings about sport. Reference (1) plus appropriate comment (1) × 2	4	▶ use of question ('But where next?') (1) suggests some uncertainty about the future (1) ▶ 'bubble' (1) suggests he thought interest in sport might disappear suddenly (1) ▶ 'tipping point' (1) suggests he felt/worried there might come a time when interest reached a high point and then declined (1) ▶ 'infatuation' (1) suggests he thought the interest in sport was overdone (1) ▶ balance of 'When I started ...' and 'Today ...' (1) shows he is comparing doubt then and confidence now (1) ▶ 'cultural giant' (1) suggests he sees sport as something huge, dominating (1) ▶ 'not a bubble' (1) is a direct rejection of his earlier worry (1) ▶ 'permanent' (1) suggests confidence in its staying power (1) ▶ balancing of '[instead of ...] aberration ... true anomaly' (1) confirms belief that sport is fundamentally important (1)

Question	Expected response	Max. mark	Additional guidance
8	You should explain in your own words three reasons why the writer refers to the Ancient Olympics to support his argument. Any three of the points in the 'Additional guidance' column for 3 marks.	3	▸ it provides him with 'the long view', e.g. looking at it over many centuries, not just a hundred or so years (1) ▸ Ancient Olympics went on for over 1,000 years, showing it was important for a long time (1) ▸ they attracted audiences/onlookers from far and wide, showing the popularity of sport (1) ▸ they were not stopped even by major issues such as war or disease (1) ▸ people were enthusiastic about them (1)
9	You should explain in your own words three reasons why, according to the writer, sport is important to us. Any three of the points in the 'Additional guidance' column for 3 marks.	3	Glosses of: ▸ 'speaks to something permanent in the human psyche', e.g. relates to deep feelings/thoughts (1) ▸ 'No amount of … will eradicate this', e.g. it can't be removed/destroyed by anything external or changed (1) ▸ 'except temporarily', e.g. if removed it will only be for a short time (1) ▸ sports 'move and inspire us', e.g. they stimulate, arouse passions, make us feel good (1) ▸ 'themes of competition … and rivalry', e.g. the key ideas of conflict and challenge (1) ▸ 'teamwork', e.g. sport encourages working together, co-operation (1) ▸ 'escape the humdrum and ordinary', e.g. get away from the dull, boring, routine (1)

Critical Reading
Section 1 – Scottish Text – 20 marks

NB The final question (for 8 marks) on each text should be marked using the general instructions below. Text-specific guidance for each final question is given at the relevant point.

You may choose to answer in **bullet** points in this final question, or write a number of linked statements. There is **no requirement** to write a 'mini-essay'.

Up to 2 marks can be achieved for identifying elements of **commonality** as identified in the question.

A further 2 marks can be achieved for **reference to the extract given**.

4 additional marks can be awarded for similar references to **at least one other text/part of the text** by the writer.

In practice this means:

Identification of commonality (2) (e.g. theme, central relationship, importance of setting, use of imagery, development in characterisation, use of personal experience, use of narrative style, or any other key element …)

from the extract:

1 × relevant reference to technique (1)
1 × appropriate comment (1)
OR
1 × relevant reference to idea (1)
1 × appropriate comment (1)
OR
1 × relevant reference to feature (1)
1 × appropriate comment (1)
OR
1 × relevant reference to text (1)
1 × appropriate comment (1)
(maximum of 2 marks only for discussion of extract)
from **at least one other text/part of the text**:
as above (× 2) for **up to 4 marks**

Part A – Scottish Text – Drama

Text 1 – Drama – Bold Girls *by Rona Munro*

Question		Expected response	Max. mark	Additional guidance
1	a	You should show how Cassie's admiration for Nora is conveyed. Reference (1) Comment (1) × 2	4	Possible answers include: ▶ 'She was something' (1) shows she is in awe, giving high praise (1) ▶ compares her with the Incredible Hulk (1) suggesting enormous strength, unstoppable when roused, on the side of right (1) ▶ 'lioness' (1) suggests power, strength, nobility (1) ▶ repeated words/single sentence 'She was.' (1) emphatic (1)

Question		Expected response	Max. mark	Additional guidance
1	b	You should explain how the dramatist conveys the liveliness of the dialogue in these lines. Each point (1)	2	Possible answers include: ▸ frequent breaking into others' speeches shows keenness to add detail (1) ▸ the way most of the interruptions are ignored, no malice detected (1) ▸ Nora's replication of Cassie's exact words/tone shows the excitement in her voice (1) ▸ Cassie's exaggerated, self-mocking description of herself ('one hand …') (1)
2		You should explain one way in which the language conveys how fast-moving the incident was. Reference (1) Comment (1) Reference could be to word choice, sentence structure, tone, etc.	2	Possible answers include: ▸ 'marched back up' (1) suggests speedy, purposeful movement (1) ▸ 'here they were' (1) suggests coming upon them suddenly, unexpectedly; suggests how imposing, menacing they were (1) ▸ 'dragging' (1) suggests hurried action (1) ▸ 'without even a pair of shoes' (1) indicates he was not given any time to get ready (1) ▸ the contrast with 'snoring … toasting … pie … can' (1) emphasises the sudden intrusion (1) ▸ repetition of 'and' (1) creates a list-like sentence emphasising how much was going on all at the same time (1) ▸ 'throwing everything every which way' (1) suggests frantic, panicky activity (1) ▸ 'all over the house' (1) suggests widespread activity (1) ▸ 'baby's screaming … child's calling' (1) suggests idea of everything happening at once (1)
3		You should explain how the dramatist creates humour in the way Cassie and Nora recall the event. Well-made point, i.e. reference (1) + explanation (1) × 2 or Basic point, i.e. reference alone or weak explanation (1) × 4	4	Possible answers include: ▸ Joe keeping his hand on the pie (1) seems bizarre in the circumstances of an arrest (1) ▸ the idea of Nora singling out the biggest RUC man (1) puts her in an amusing light as the battling little woman (1) ▸ the 'mountain/beetle' comparison (1) is greatly exaggerated for comic effect (1) ▸ Cassie's 'Can you beat it, Marie?' (1) invites us to see the absurdity of the confrontation (1) ▸ Nora's use of 'bastard' (1) after complaining moments earlier about Cassie's language (1) ▸ the suddenness of the soldier's response ('Wallop') (1) given Nora's challenge not to strike a woman (1) ▸ 'straight through the hedge' (1) suggests amusing, cartoon-like image (1) ▸ Nora's self-deprecating 'Sure I got my answer …' (2) ▸ 'Choked on her false teeth' might be literally true, but has humour in the indignity of mentioning such an item (2)

Question	Expected response	Max. mark	Additional guidance
3 (continued)			▶ 'Mummy in the hedge with her little legs waving in the air' (1) suggests loss of dignity (after her previous self-confidence) (1) ▶ 'oh but that was a terrible night' (1) said while crying with laughter is amusing in itself (1)
4	You should show how the women's lives are affected by 'The Troubles'. Reference could be made to the following: ▶ the death of Michael ▶ imprisonment of Joe (and Davey and Martin) ▶ taken to wedding in an armoured car ▶ disruption to daily lives by road blocks, searches, raids ▶ damage to bamboo suite by Army in pursuit of suspect ▶ frequent sounds of gunfire off-stage – little attention is paid by the women ▶ the raid at the Club ▶ the silence at the Club for a dead IRA man (a regular event)	8	Marks for this question should be allocated following the guidelines given at the start of these Marking Instructions.

Text 2 – Drama – Sailmaker *by Alan Spence*

Question	Expected response	Max. mark	Additional guidance
5	You should identify four ways by which the dramatist makes it clear that Alec is annoyed with his father. Four points from the Additional guidance column for 1 mark each.	4	Possible answers include: ▶ says as little as possible/doesn't elaborate on anything he says (1) ▶ doesn't look up when father speaks (1) ▶ one-word response 'Aye' (1) ▶ minimal/monosyllabic response: 'A book' (1) ▶ very clipped 'Got an exam next week' (1) ▶ impatient response 'That's what ah said' (1) ▶ has to force out his 'Thanks' for the crisps and Irn Bru (1) ▶ unmoved by his father's attempt to cheer him up by singing (1) ▶ dismissive, slightly aggressive 'Chuck it will ye!' (1)

Question	Expected response	Max. mark	Additional guidance
6	You should explain how the way Davie speaks is typical of someone who is slightly drunk. Reference (1) Comment/Explanation (1) × 2	4	Possible answers include: ▸ 'Och …' (1) suggests he can't think clearly enough to offer an explanation or doesn't think his son's concerns are important (1) ▸ 'Just … wan a these things' (1) is a rather incoherent (or irresponsible) response (1) ▸ the self-justification (1) of claims like 'Nae harm … Didnae even have a lot …' (1) ▸ 'Wee refreshment' (1) typical, clichéd attempt to diminish the scale of what he's done (1) ▸ enthusiastic recitation of Burns (1) is reminiscent of the poem itself (1) ▸ 'Great stuff eh?' (1) trying to cajole a response from someone who's not interested (1) ▸ the repetition of 'Reamin swats' (1) as if he's in a dream world (1) ▸ 'Anythin for eatin?' (1) sudden change of subject suggests a rather confused mind (1)
7	You should show how the tension between Alec and his father is conveyed by the way they speak. Reference (1) Comment/Explanation (1) × 2	4	Possible answers include: ▸ series of questions and short responses (1) indicates a less than friendly exchange (1) ▸ the extreme brevity of Alec's responses (1) suggests he is unwilling to have any sort of conversation with his father (1) ▸ the absence of any apology/contrition in Alec's responses (1) suggests he is quite content to offend/punish his father (1) ▸ Alec's failure to respond to the promise of steak and chips (1) suggests the depth of his antagonism (1) ▸ Alec's reaction to Davie's mention of Peggy by banging down the book (1) shows he is angered/disgusted at his father's behaviour (1)
8	You should show how you are led to believe whether or not Davie is a good parent. You should discuss whether Davie is a good parent or not. They can argue for either side or for both. Reference could be made to the following: **Bad qualities:** ▸ his drinking ▸ his gambling ▸ his irresponsibility with money ▸ his constant 'something will turn up … we havnae died a winter' philosophy ▸ his lack of drive/ambition	8	Marks for this question should be allocated following the guidelines given at the start of these Marking Instructions.

Question	Expected response	Max. mark	Additional guidance
8 (continued)	**Good qualities:** ▸ his obvious affection for his son ▸ his support of his son's education ▸ he tries to temper the sectarianism of Billy and Ian ▸ he doesn't criticise Alec's religious phase, even though he seems to disapprove		

Text 3 – Drama – Tally's Blood by Ann Marie Di Mambro

Question	Expected response	Max. mark	Additional guidance
9	You should explain how the language used conveys Rosinella's hostility towards Lucia. Reference (1) Comment/explanation (1) × 2	4	Possible answers include: ▸ the repeated use of 'eh?' (1) suggests impatience (1) ▸ the two questions in first speech (1) both short, slightly aggressive (1) ▸ 'I knew it' (1) as if she's outsmarted Lucia (1) ▸ repetition of 'What's it say?'/'Read it.' (1) demanding, unforgiving tone (1) ▸ use of imperatives (1) shows her as forceful (1)
10	You should explain how the way Lucia speaks makes it clear she is making up a story on the spot. Reference (1) Comment/explanation (1) × 2	4	Possible answers include: ▸ frequent ellipses (1) suggest pauses to think (1) ▸ repetition of 'it just says' (1) suggests she's padding it out (1) ▸ 'and eh' (1) suggests she can't think what to say next (1) ▸ 'So he does … and so do I … as well … I think so too' (1) empty words, flailing attempt to keep going (1) ▸ 'No, it is good' (1) by deliberately misunderstanding Rosinella's comment she gets a chance to cause a distraction (1) ▸ singing the song lyric (1) means she is relieved of the pressure to make anything up (1)
11	You should explain how Rosinella's language makes clear her low opinion of Hughie. Reference (1) Comment/explanation (1) × 2	4	Possible answers include: ▸ the use of 'that' in 'that Hughie Devlin' (1) sounds contemptuous, as if he were part of some lesser breed (1) ▸ repeated pattern of 'I don't want you seeing him … I don't want you talking to him …' (1) suggests he is to be avoided at all costs (1) ▸ refusal to engage in any of Lucia's defences of him (1) suggests she doesn't think he's worth discussing (1) ▸ 'get rid of' (1) likens him almost to vermin to be eradicated (1) ▸ 'Jumped up wee piece of nothing' (1) shows she thinks he is worthless and/or is getting above his station (1) ▸ 'Him?' (1) reduces him to a sneering monosyllable (1) ▸ 'the likes of him' (1) suggests she sees him as a type, not as a person (1)

Question	Expected response	Max. mark	Additional guidance
12	You should show how the relationship between Lucia and Hughie develops. Reference could be made to the following: ▸ initially 'forced' together to improve Lucia's English ▸ at first, Lucia is a little disdainful of him/teases him ▸ they become good 'play' friends (play at schools; blood brothers) though Lucia always has the upper hand ▸ grow together naturally ▸ Hughie is unable to express his love ▸ gift of penknife; the hug ▸ Hughie follows her to Italy ▸ the 'Elopement' and happy ending	8	Marks for this question should be allocated following the guidelines given at the start of these Marking Instructions.

Part B – Scottish Text – Prose

Text 1 – Prose – The Cone-Gatherers *by Robin Jenkins*

Question	Expected response	Max. mark	Additional guidance
13	You should show how the writer's use of language creates a dramatic scene. Reference (1) Comment (1) × 2	4	Possible answers include: ▸ the contrast between 'petrified' and 'leaping out' (1) creates a vivid picture of differing reactions (1) ▸ 'petrified' (1) suggests absolute terror, shock (1) ▸ 'leaping out' (1) suggests surprising, unexpected movement (1) ▸ paradoxical/contradictory phrase 'berserk joy' (1) suggests confused, irrational, out of control (1) ▸ short, blunt sentence 'There was a knife in his hand' (1) abruptly focuses attention on instrument of destruction (1) ▸ colon after 'shouted to him' (1) introduces the disturbing detail that she didn't even know what she was shouting/ that Duror was not in a state to hear her (1) ▸ 'rushing upon …' (1) suggests frantic, uncontrolled action (1) ▸ 'furious force' (1) suggests frenzied, aggressive movement (1) ▸ alliteration in 'furious force' (1) emphasises the ferocity of the attack (1) ▸ 'savagely' (1) conveys the violence, brutality of the attack (1) ▸ sequence of five short sentences from 'Blood …' onwards (1) unelaborated to convey the stark horror, like a sequence of shocking photographs (1)

Question	Expected response	Max. mark	Additional guidance
14	You should explain in your own words what makes Duror's behaviour appear to be out of the ordinary. Each point (1) × 4	4	Possible answers include: ▶ he stays on the ground with the dead deer (1) ▶ he looks as if he's grieving over it (1) ▶ he doesn't let go of the knife (1) ▶ his speech is incoherent (1) ▶ he keeps eyes closed (1) ▶ he looks drunk (1) ▶ his mouth is hanging open (1) ▶ he appears like a simpleton (1)
15	You should explain what impressions the writer creates of Lady Runcie-Campbell. Impression (1) Reference/explanation (1) × 2	4	Possible answers include: ▶ accepts role of leader (1) 'came forward' (1) ▶ can't help showing her disapproval (1) 'involuntary grimaces of distaste' (1) ▶ tries to distance herself from anything unpleasant (1) 'avoided looking at the hunchback' (1) ▶ concern for welfare of employees (1) 'Has he hurt himself?' (1) ▶ rather detached, aloof (1) 'Has he hurt himself?'/refers to Duror in the third person (1) ▶ formality of speech/ease of giving command (1) 'please be so good as to …' (1) ▶ expects others to jump to her command (1) saying 'Have we nothing to wipe his face with?' (1) ▶ irritated by trivial detail (1) 'peevishly' (1)
16	You should show how the writer creates a contrast between Calum and Duror. Reference could be made to the following: ▶ essentially a contrast between good and evil ▶ physically opposite: Calum is deformed; Duror is passed physically fit by Dr Matheson ▶ emotionally opposite: Calum is caring, compassionate; Duror is vicious, destructive ▶ psychologically opposite: Calum has childlike innocence; Duror has adult prejudices ▶ Calum is always referred to by first name; Duror by his surname ▶ Calum can't bring himself to kill the injured rabbit; Duror does it with ease	8	Marks for this question should be allocated following the guidelines given at the start of these Marking Instructions.

Question	Expected response	Max. mark	Additional guidance
16 (*continued*)	▸ in Lendrick: Duror is isolated; Calum is accepted by others ▸ the echoes at the end of Calum as Christ (dead in the tree) and Duror as Judas (going off to kill himself)		

Text 2 – Prose – The Testament of Gideon Mack *by James Robertson*

Question	Expected response	Max. mark	Additional guidance
17	You should show how the writer's language illustrates the idea that Gideon is in a 'crisis'. Reference (1) Comment (1) × 2	4	Possible answers include: ▸ 'sweating' (1) suggests stress, pressure (1) ▸ 'seething with energy' (1) suggests inner turmoil, hyperactive (1) ▸ 'energy would burst out' (1) suggests dangerous eruption of activity (1) ▸ 'wrecked' (1) suggests he would be in a drained, damaged state (1) ▸ 'twitching' (1) suggests he is making involuntary movements (1) ▸ 'as if in contact with an electric fence' (1) imagines some external force is controlling him (1) ▸ contradiction of 'wanted to go … was afraid to go' (1) indicates the turmoil in his mind (1) ▸ personification of the Stone (1) suggests irrational train of thought (1) ▸ 'paced' (1) suggests agitated, stressed movement (1) ▸ 'in and out … up and down' (1) structure suggests random, frenzied movement (1) ▸ 'rushed to the front door' (1) suggests lack of control, desperate to speak to Elsie (1)
18	You should explain two impressions the reader is given of Lorna's character. Aspect of character (1) Reference/supporting evidence (1) × 2	4	Possible answers include: ▸ brisk/no-nonsense person (1) gets straight to the point about her museum visit, no introductory chatter (1) ▸ sensitive (1) notices Gideon's expression, asks if it's a bad time (1) ▸ not easily put off (1) many possible references: e.g. talks over Gideon's attempt to speak, remains insistent about going to Black Jaws, gives several reasons for going to Black Jaws, etc. (1) ▸ manipulative (1) looks 'pleadingly' at Gideon (1) ▸ possibly capable of manic behaviour (1) 'I imagined her scraping and chapping at the windows' (1)

Question	Expected response	Max. mark	Additional guidance
19	You should show that Gideon's thinking is both rational and irrational. Each point (1) × 4	4	Possible answers include: Rational: ▸ makes a clear decision (1) ▸ plans a definite course of action (1) ▸ logical approach ('If … then …' formula) (1) ▸ accepts that Elsie may be right/that he may need help (1) Irrational: ▸ prepared to believe that the Stone could be influencing events (1) ▸ prepared to believe in supernatural powers of the Stone (1) ▸ something almost hysterical in 'confront them with the misery and mockery of our lives' (1)
20	You should show how the writer explores Gideon's relationships with women. Reference could be made to the following: ▸ Jenny: quiet courtship (spurred on by Elsie); her attitude to Gideon becoming a minister; marriage; contentedness; effect of her death ▸ Elsie: early friendship in Edinburgh; admires her liveliness (finds Jenny more introspective); fantasises about her after Jenny's death; the sexual encounter; her belief that he needs help ▸ Catherine Craigie: fascinated by her; drawn to her as a fellow non-conformist; admires her outspokenness ▸ Lorna Sprott: a fellow eccentric; finds her irritating, but doesn't dislike her ▸ mother: (when young) pities her because of how his father treats her; (when older) feelings about putting her in home, phones rather than visits ▸ Amelia Wishaw: rather intimidated by her	8	Marks for this question should be allocated following the guidelines given at the start of these Marking Instructions.

Question	Expected response	Max. mark	Additional guidance
			▶ (imagery of) 'as if the air itself' (1) suggests something supernatural (1)
			▶ 'vision' (1) suggests something almost spiritual (1)
28	You should explain two ways in which the language used creates a tense mood. Reference (1) Comment/explanation (1) × 2	4	Possible answers include: ▶ the series/list of questions (1) suggests their uncertainty (1) ▶ word choice of 'clutching' (1) shows the elder to be behaving oddly/in a heightened state (1) ▶ 'like a man in a daze' (1) suggests they perceive him as behaving in a peculiar way/in a way they can't understand (1) ▶ 'turning away from each other' (1) suggests strained atmosphere between them (1) ▶ 'parted … without speaking' (1) absence of normal civilities suggests something is out of the ordinary (1) ▶ the fat woman's hesitation/uncertainty after leaving (1) suggests she is confused/nervous (1) ▶ (relatively) short sentences throughout (1) suggests lack of engagement, basic details, staccato delivery (1)
29	You should show how Crichton Smith ends his stories in a surprising or thought-provoking way. Reference could be made to the following: ▶ **The Telegram:** the tension between the two women is unexpectedly relieved when the elder passes both houses; the twist at end when it is revealed that the telegram is for the elder himself ▶ **Home:** after the visit to their old home, with its occasional nostalgia on the man's part, the couple feel completely at home among the rich and influential; the thought-provoking idea that the ambience of this hotel in the West of Scotland is 'much like Africa' ▶ **Mother and Son:** a shocking and disturbing ending as the son appears ready to attack/kill the mother; made dramatic/enigmatic because the story ends before any such act takes place	8	Marks for this question should be allocated following the guidelines given at the start of these Marking Instructions.